To the animals.

*The mission of Storey Publishing is to serve our customers by
publishing practical information that encourages
personal independence in harmony with the environment.*

Edited by Hannah Fries
Art direction and book design by Bredna Lago
Text production by Jennifer Jepson Smith
Illustrations by © Daniela Gallego

Storey books may be purchased in bulk for business, educational, or promotional use. Special editions or book excerpts can also be created to specification. For details, please contact your local bookseller or the Hachette Book Group Special Markets Department at special.markets@hbgusa.com.

Storey Publishing
210 MASS MoCA Way
North Adams, MA 01247
storey.com

Storey Publishing is an imprint of Workman Publishing, a division of Hachette Book Group, Inc., 1290 Avenue of the Americas, New York, NY 10104. The Storey Publishing name and logo are registered trademarks of Hachette Book Group, Inc.

ISBNs: 978-1-63586-856-2 (hardcover with ribbon marker); 978-1-63586-857-9 (ebook)

Printed in China by R. R. Donnelley on paper from responsible sources
10 9 8 7 6 5 4 3 2 1

APS

Library of Congress Cataloging-in-Publication Data on file

THE
GIFT
OF
ANIMALS

Poems
of Love, Loss, and Connection

Edited by **ALISON HAWTHORNE DEMING**

Foreword by **Robin Wall Kimmerer**

Storey Publishing

CONTENTS

COMPANIONSHIP

FEAR and VULNERABILITY

THE LEAST AMONG US

THE SACRED

THE FUTURE OF ANIMALS

On Giving & Receiving

A few dark winters ago, I began a practice of hand-feeding the chickadees in the snowy woods. They brought me so much joy, I wanted to give them something in return. I treasured our shared observations of one another, the mutual curiosity and, eventually, the thrilling feel of their scaly little feet wrapped around my freezing finger. But more than that, I found myself yearning for a glance of recognition from the being behind that bright obsidian eye. It was a biophilic desire to see and be seen. With seeds in my open palm, I understood that this was not just about feeding them—they were feeding me, with the gifts of animals.

In the remembrances of my Potawatomi culture, the old people said that there was a long-ago time when all the people, human and otherwise, spoke the same language. We shared teachings and warnings and everyday gossip about the doings of our neighbors. But, no more. We've been cut off, although most humans don't even recollect the loss, except in rare moments of interspecies encounter. The poems in this collection provide such moments, fleeting glimpses of deep connection.

Interpreting our estrangement from the natural world, ecopsychologists have suggested that modern humans suffer from an ailment that author Michael Vincent McGinnis calls "species loneliness." We grieve the moments of awe, the chance to learn from intelligences other than our own, and we crave the mutual respect we once enjoyed. Species loneliness is a gulf that people try to cross in diverse ways, through animal companions and wildlife viewing, and in misguided ways, such as tourists who force themselves on wild bison for a selfie. This gorgeous collection of encounters feels like an antidote to species loneliness, providing a multifaceted lens on our desire for communion with the more-than-human world.

These pages also embody mindful humility regarding the limits to our understanding of animal lives. As editor, Alison Hawthorne Deming reminds us: Their view of the world is not ours, and the things they know and sense are invisible to us. These vibrant encounters recognize our dual impulses to be in intimate relations with animal beings and, at the same time, to respect their intrinsic autonomy from the human-dominated world. In visits with buffalo, manatees, ants, and frogs, we experience a stretching back and forth between awe for the sovereignty and profound otherness of animal lives and glimpses of a not-quite-forgotten kinship that stirs the recognition that we are not alone, whether that animal being is purring in our lap or is glimpsed through the forest at the edge of our shaded consciousness.

In this time of the Sixth Extinction, the species being lost mount like a pile of bleached bones. In the face of such tragedy and complicity, these poems stir something deeply reciprocal in our animal memory. They do so by celebrating all the particular ways of being across the taxa, from languid cats to javelinas, roaches, lynx, and minks.

For the joy that animals give us, we are called to give our gifts in return, from an open palm of sunflower seeds to the luminous book in your hands.

—ROBIN WALL KIMMERER

Animals & the Creative Spirit

All my life I have loved animals. I grew up with Bear, the golden retriever, and Tiger, the tabby cat, with chipmunks who raced in the hickory trees of our Connecticut woods, lambs and horses and chickens I cared for in my Vermont years, bobcats and roadrunners who visited my backyard in my Arizona years, elephants I met in a zoo where I helped to install a poetry path, finbacks and dolphins lacing through the Bay of Fundy with the mystical grace of gods.

All my life I have feared animals. I was attacked by two dogs as a young child, and, though I have great affection for canines and currently live with a 70-pound goldendoodle, an aggressive growler can make me leap in fear. I am not keen on rattlesnakes, though they have been cordial in announcing their presence and teaching me my place. I am not keen on being stalked by a cougar or rushed by a grizzly protecting her cubs. In fact, I chickened out of a hike in Alaska after seeing a very fresh and very large bear track in the mud.

All my life I have grieved over animals. Pets dying, entire species dying, all those wild things lost to roadkill, the anguish of the predator-prey dance. And I have come to see that grief as a measure of my love. I have marveled at the least among us, the little beauties that abound in the insect world, even the vast population of microbes that inhabit my body and make my life possible. I have envied cultures in which animals are held sacred, earning reverence and gratitude. I have celebrated the spiritual feeling toward animals that arises with a close encounter. I have slipped into thought experiments about the future: How will our marvelously inventive planet handle the destructive changes we have inflicted upon it? What new species might evolve? If dinosaurs evolved over eons to become the birds that visit our

backyards, what astonishments of evolutionary invention might lie ahead? How will the sheer force of life assert itself in the decades and centuries and millennia to come?

Tracy K. Smith writes, "I take solace in the fact that it's poems we turn to for moments of big change." Surely, poems will bring that solace to our contemplation of animals in this time of change, too.

I know I am not alone in feeling this complex range of emotions when I think about animals. The human-animal connection is profound, beautiful, and troubling. This anthology celebrates our ability to capture such emotional complexity in poems, renewing an appreciation for how deeply we are connected to our animal kin, whether domestic or wild, and reminding us that the presence of animals in our lives is a gift.

The diverse voices gathered here speak to our collective urge to bear witness to the lives of animals, to find solace in their companionship, to wonder at their beauty and intelligence, to empathize over their suffering, and to hope for their future. They remind us that animals have the power to stir the full range of human emotions: love, happiness, sadness, fear, anger, disgust, and wonder.

This connection between humans and animals stretches far into our past. The earliest art, found in cave paintings and sculptures that date back 40 thousand years, features animals prominently. There are very few images of human beings, other than the ochre handprints that served as the artist's signature. Animals were once at the center of the human story.

In fact, for most of human history, people lived in close proximity to animals. Animals gave us our food and clothing, our myths and our sense of the sacred. Now in our urban, industrialized, and virtual worlds, our interactions with creatures are diminished. Many of us long for animal encounters that can spur and quicken the heart.

When I wrote the book *Zoologies: On Animals and the Human Spirit*, I looked for animal stories that made me feel wonderstruck, as I did in childhood. I was tired of hearing the sad summary of loss, the depressing data about the fate of animals. I wanted to engage with animal presence, to feel the spiritual force of animals. I wanted to feel animals invite me into continuity and connection with forces larger than myself. I wanted my readers to feel wonder at the marvels of the animal world. I wrote a praise song to a spider, a lament for the suffering of African elephants, an elegy for a house cat, a reflection on chimeras in both myth and science, a love story for the northern spotted owl. I wanted twenty-first-century animal stories, and I found them everywhere. The more stories I told, the more people gave me their stories. Animals, it would appear, still move the creative spirit.

This anthology turns to contemporary poets to continue that exploration. The book is organized into seven sections: Praise, Lament, Companionship, Fear and Vulnerability, the Least Among Us, the Sacred, and the Future of Animals. Each section is introduced by a poem from an older tradition, an Echo, giving voice to diverse cultural traditions and perspectives on the human-animal connection. My hope is that the poems spark a deeper appreciation for every creature who inhabits these pages: horse, lark, koala, fox, sloth, cricket, octopus, dog, coyote, worm, chimera, cockroach, lion, mammoth, eagle, snake, cat, microbe, nightjar . . . and more. My hope is that the poems inspire our biophilia—the human capacity to love and care for our animal relations.

—ALISON HAWTHORNE DEMING

PRAISE

P raise is an expression of admiration and love, a feeling that lifts us out of the ordinary and into the extraordinary. We invite animals to share our homes. We carry photos of our pets on our cell phones. We geek out on videos of interspecies friendships: cheetah and golden retriever, cat and parakeet, coyote and badger, duckling and lamb. The Bible invites us to praise the moment when the lion lies down with the lamb. The Psalms praise "all creatures great and small." In Buddhist tradition, all animals are sentient beings, worthy of respect and care.

One measure of our love for animals is the surprising fact that more Americans visit zoos than professional athletic events. Clearly, we love animals, and we love to sing their praises. The connection between people and animals is long and deep. They gentle us. They remind us that beauty is nature's language, and she is eloquent.

Praise poems are among the oldest poetic traditions. They express love and gratitude. Yoruba praise poems are sung by a hunter to an animal he seeks. The Baka people of Gabon envision a unity of animals in motion with their chant: "All lives, all dances, and all is loud!" Contemporary poems bring this tradition into our moment: the girl who learns her strengths from a horse, the urban dog who trots along confident in his street smarts, the man who finds his own tenderness in kissing a horse, the gratitude expressed to elephants who helped clean up the mess after a disastrous tsunami, the Affrilachian grandfather who recognizes a wildness that can't be tamed.

From the Oral Tradition of the Inuit

The poet Edward Field translated text recorded by the Danish explorer Knud Rasmussen on his 1921 expedition to the Arctic. Rasmussen had lived among the Inuit, collecting songs and stories from their oral tradition. When Field read these works, he was inspired to translate them into English and write poems after the originals.

Nalungiaq was an elderly Inuit woman who reported that she had learned the song "Magic Words" from her uncle Unaraluk, who was a shaman. The poem is an echo coming from deep time, passed from generation to generation, an act of praise for a transcendent vision of the spiritual connection between people and animals.

MAGIC WORDS

from the Inuit, after Nalungiaq

In the very earliest time,
when both people and animals lived on earth,
a person could become an animal if he wanted to and an animal
could become a human being.
Sometimes they were people
and sometimes animals
and there was no difference.
All spoke the same language.
That was the time when words were like magic.
The human mind had mysterious powers.
A word spoken by chance
might have strange consequences.
It would suddenly come alive
and what people wanted to happen could happen—
all you had to do was say it.
Nobody could explain this:
That's just the way it was.

Ada Limón

HOW TO TRIUMPH LIKE A GIRL

I like the lady horses best,
how they make it all look easy,
like running 40 miles per hour
is as fun as taking a nap, or grass.
I like their lady horse swagger,
after winning. Ears up, girls, ears up!
But mainly, let's be honest, I like
that they're ladies. As if this big
dangerous animal is also a part of me,
that somewhere inside the delicate
skin of my body, there pumps
an 8-pound female horse heart,
giant with power, heavy with blood.
Don't you want to believe it?
Don't you want to lift my shirt and see
the huge beating genius machine
that thinks, no, it knows,
it's going to come in first.

ODE TO THE FISH

Nights when I can't sleep, I listen to the sea lions
barking from the rocks off the lighthouse.
I look out the black window into the black night
and think about fish stirring the oceans.
Muscular tuna, their lunge and thrash
churning the water, whipping up a squall,
storm of hunger. Herring cruising,
river of silver in the sea, wide as a lit city.
And all the small breaths: pulse
of frilled jellyfish, thrust of squid,
frenzy of krill, transparent skin glowing
green with the glass shells of diatoms.
Billions swarming up the water column each night,
gliding down at dawn. They're the greased motor
that powers the world. Shipping heat
to the arctic, hauling cold to the tropics,
currents unspooling around the globe.
My room is so still, the bureau lifeless,
and on it, inert, the paraphernalia of humans:
keys, coins, shells that once rocked in the tides—
opalescent abalone, pearl earrings.
Only the clock's sea-green numerals
register small changes. And shadows
the moon casts—fan of maple branches—
tick across the room. But beyond the cliffs
a blue whale sounds and surfaces, cosmic
ladle scooping the icy depths. An artery so wide,
I could swim through into its thousand-pound heart.

ELEPHANTS

I think of the elephants
who gave rides to children,
lifted them up with their trunks
and carried them to higher ground,

tuskers, lifting roof beams
and cement markers,
clearing rubbish
after the waves retired—

what reward
do they deserve?
One hundred acres of pure
second growth forest,

certified, that will not
be tilled or cut?
How about liberation
on the city streets,

a weekend pass?
I suggest we trust
that nobody
will be trampled,

that we've taken
the necessary
precautions
to let our fellow animals

roam freely among us.
Let's put these
elephants on a stage:
marvels, heroes among men.

WILD GRATITUDE

Tonight when I knelt down next to our cat, Zooey,
And put my fingers into her clean cat's mouth,
And rubbed her swollen belly that will never know kittens,
And watched her wriggle onto her side, pawing the air,
And listened to her solemn little squeals of delight,
I was thinking about the poet, Christopher Smart,
Who wanted to kneel down and pray without ceasing
In every one of the splintered London streets,

And was locked away in the madhouse at St. Luke's
With his sad religious mania, and his wild gratitude,
And his grave prayers for the other lunatics,
And his great love for his speckled cat, Jeoffry.
All day today—August 13, 1983—I remembered how
Christopher Smart blessed this same day in August, 1759,
For its calm bravery and ordinary good conscience.

This was the day that he blessed the Postmaster General
"And all conveyancers of letters" for their warm humanity,
And the gardeners for their private benevolence
And intricate knowledge of the language of flowers,
And the milkmen for their universal human kindness.
This morning I understood that he loved to hear—
As I have heard—the soft clink of milk bottles
On the rickety stairs in the early morning,

And how terrible it must have seemed
When even this small pleasure was denied him.
But it wasn't until tonight when I knelt down
And slipped my hand into Zooey's waggling mouth
That I remembered how he'd called Jeoffry "the servant
Of the Living God duly and daily serving Him,"
And for the first time understood what it meant.
Because it wasn't until I saw my own cat

Whine and roll over on her fluffy back
That I realized how gratefully he had watched
Jeoffry fetch and carry his wooden cork
Across the grass in the wet garden, patiently
Jumping over a high stick, calmly sharpening
His claws on the woodpile, rubbing his nose
Against the nose of another cat, stretching, or
Slowly stalking his traditional enemy, the mouse,
A rodent, "a creature of great personal valour,"
And then dallying so much that his enemy escaped.

And only then did I understand
It is Jeoffry—and every creature like him—
Who can teach us how to praise—purring
In their own language,
Wreathing themselves in the living fire.

THE LARK'S NEST

From yon black clump of wheat that grows
  More rank and higher than the rest
A lark—I marked her as she rose—
  At early morning left her nest.
Her eggs were four of dusky hue
  Blotched brown as is the very ground
With tinges of a purply hue
  The larger ends encircling round.

Behind a clod how snug the nest
  Is in a horse's footing fixed!
Of twitch and stubbles roughly dressed
  With roots and horsehair intermixed.
The wheat surrounds it like a bower
  And like to thatch each bowing blade
Throws off the frequent falling shower
—And here's an egg this morning laid!

KISSING A HORSE

Of the two spoiled, barn-sour geldings
we owned that year, it was Red—
skittish and prone to explode
even at fourteen years—who'd let me
hold to my face his own: the massive labyrinthine
caverns of the nostrils, the broad plain
up the head to the eyes. He'd let me stroke
his coarse chin whiskers and take
his soft meaty underlip
in my hands, press my man's carnivorous
kiss to his grass-nipping upper half of one, just
so that I could smell
the long way his breath had come from the rain
and the sun, the lungs and the heart,
from a world that meant no harm.

THE WATER WITCH ON SALVATION

When the horses took off with the wagon
and my grandbaby inside, I chased it.
My legs nigh on seventy, moved like a lightening twenty—
down the bank and across the pasture,
I hollered out, "Hah up now!"
and old Trigger stopped,
stood stiff and straight, real proud,
cutting his black eyes at me like he was saying
"You old somebitch, I showed you."
I lifted the baby out, rested her on the ground—safe.
The baby took my finger; she didn't cry a lick.
We left the wagon, walked the horse back to the barn,
then that girl breaks my grip and runs; she runs, she runs
through the pasture, up the hill, as if nothing happened at all.
Not a tear a one, nare one sign of being scared.
The nip in the morning made me think of old hog killing times,
made me think of Old Man Pat,
who'd rather see the fresh chittlins rot on the ground,
than me take em home to feed my younguns.
I felt old Trigger's breath on my hand, warm and stank.
I pat his flank and we're back to being friends.
The hurtin in my knee comes back on me like a toothache,
made me wonder if any beast living could ever be tamed.

KOALAS

Hammocked in the forest's high
hush. Tucked away from the gnawing
need for approval. Eucalyptus, company
enough. Koalas, only social for 15 minutes

a day, don't need to convince the world
to keep them. Koalas would rather sleep
than spend energy looking
for a mate. Koala, meaning "no water."

What's it like to be that thirstless? To not crave
the slow sips of a stranger's gaze, the want
to be wanted. To say I'm the only one

worth my time. Invite the satisfaction
of single. Autonomy, under-
appreciated view. Alone at night,
they sit, watch the holy saint
of solitude, sink sunset. Just look at her
power, how she turns her back
and the whole sky
speaks red.

DOG

The dog trots freely in the street
and sees reality
and the things he sees
are bigger than himself
and the things he sees
are his reality
Drunks in doorways
Moons on trees
The dog trots freely thru the street
and the things he sees
are smaller than himself
Fish on newsprint
Ants in holes
Chickens in Chinatown windows
their heads a block away
The dog trots freely in the street
and the things he smells
smell something like himself
The dog trots freely in the street
past puddles and babies
cats and cigars
poolrooms and policemen
He doesn't hate cops
He merely has no use for them
and he goes past them
and past the dead cows hung up whole
in front of the San Francisco Meat Market
He would rather eat a tender cow

than a tough policeman
though either might do
And he goes past the Romeo Ravioli Factory
and past Coit's Tower
and past Congressman Doyle
He's afraid of Coit's Tower
but he's not afraid of Congressman Doyle
although what he hears is very discouraging
very depressing
very absurd
to a sad young dog like himself
to a serious dog like himself
But he has his own free world to live in
His own fleas to eat
He will not be muzzled
Congressman Doyle is just another
fire hydrant
to him
The dog trots freely in the street
and has his own dog's life to live
and to think about
and to reflect upon
touching and tasting and testing everything
investigating everything
without benefit of perjury
a real realist
with a real tale to tell
and a real tail to tell it with
a real live

                    barking
                                democratic dog
engaged in real
                    free enterprise
with something to say
                    about ontology
something to say
            about reality
                    and how to see it
                                and how to hear it
with his head cocked sideways
                        at streetcorners
as if he is just about to have
                    his picture taken
                                for Victor Records
            listening for
                    His Master's Voice
            and looking
                    like a living questionmark
                                into the
                        great gramophone
                        of puzzling existence
            with its wondrous hollow horn
                which always seems
            just about to spout forth
                            some Victorious answer
                            to everything

LOVE POEM: CHIMERA

I thought myself lion and serpent. Thought
myself body enough for two, for we.
Found comfort in never being lonely.

What burst from my back, from my bones, what lived
along the ridge from crown to crown, from mane
to forked tongue beneath the skin. What clamor

we made in the birthing. What hiss and rumble
at the splitting, at the horns and beard,
at the glottal bleat. What bridges our back.

What strong neck, what bright eye. What menagerie
are we. What we've made of ourselves.

CANTO FOR THE CHESTNUT-EARED LAUGHINGTHRUSH

And then rushed into the embrace of the mountains
Of the Kontum Plateau, ferried through Lo Xo pass,
Blew past Măng Đen, dizzied among hairpin turns,
Floating in the lushness 1,200m above sea level,
Amid a mosaic of prime evergreen, gasping.
And up there we saw: strata of emerald forms,
Of beech, laurel, magnolia, heather, and myrtle.
Under unbroken canopy, in the undergrowth
Of that species rich upper montane wet forest,
Hidden somewhere in that mystery must be
Our very own Chestnut-eared Laughingthrush.
Garrulax konkakinhensis was our day's journey
And query, who appeared in our dreams calling.
So we began our search, checked known locations.
At the first spot, magpies. The next: babblers.
But we kept looking, listening, knowing the forest
Gives up its secrets slowly. And passion we knew
From experience associates with wild patience.
On our lips the other name, *Khướu Kon Ka Kính,*
For the shy terrestrial bird who has no need for names,
But sustenance and song. Then came a rasping buzz.
Close by us, there in the undergrowth, a voice
Signed among the trees. A few turns of the
Kaleidoscope, new shapes and colors rearranged
Themselves into the winged creature we sought out:
Brown and black dappled, spotted, and speckled,
The chestnut patch brushed behind the knowing eye,

Blurring well into the daylight world of shadows.
As if a slight breeze stirred, gentle movements
Among the leaves and branches told us our bird
Retreated out of sight. We all breathed again.
The laughingthrush exists. The mountain forest exists.
This was only prelude, for we struck deeper into
The interior seeking greater clarity, closer listening.
And so we stood like trees staring back into the trees,
Ears peering through the green abundance,
Touching the colorful cacophony of sounds.
Reader, desire follows you into the field,
Where what you want colors what you see.
On the road back to Pleiku, looking out across
The highlands that held us, we all smiled—
There was no need for words. Each replayed
In their mind's eye the day's loveliness.
Then came news of extinction. The Javan rhino
Dead, the last of his kind found slaughtered
At Cát Tiên, horn sawed off. Joy fell from the sky.
Let us not tell our children a story that begins,
Once in the forests there was a laughingthrush . . .
We had met with Chestnut-eared Laughingthrush
Again and again, there in the heart of the heart
Of the forest, there where our fellow humans
Had not cleared, hunted, trapped, and defoliated
Life out of existence. There sweet thrush-like notes
May stream yet as water over rows of stones.
Others there sang the songs of their species too.
And our bodies also lighter with laughter.

the earth is a living thing

is a black shambling bear
ruffling its wild back and tossing
mountains into the sea

is a black hawk circling
the burying ground circling the bones
picked clean and discarded

is a fish black blind in the belly of water
is a diamond blind in the black belly of coal

is a black and living thing
is a favorite child
of the universe
feel her rolling her hand
in its kinky hair
feel her brushing it clean

LAMENT

Grief can level us. The loss of a loved one, human or animal, can take a profound physical and emotional toll on our well-being. Where do we turn for consolation? Poetry does not shy away from such feelings. Rather, poetry welcomes our grief and sorrow and can transform it into elegy, lament, and recollection of the beloved brought near through imagination. Poetry bears witness to absence. It creates a vessel to contain our grief. And in paying attention to what is lost, it honors the dead.

Animals, too, experience grief. Elephants bury the bones of their dead and return years later to touch them. The orca Tahlequah became famous around the world when she carried her stillborn calf aloft in water off the Pacific coast for 17 days. Poems about the grief suffered by animals educate our empathy—they teach us to care. They teach us that we are not alone in our sorrow.

Grief is a measure of our love. With the diminishment of the animal world and the generational trauma of history, we have invented new registers of grief and new challenges in bearing witness. Kimberly Blaeser rises to this challenge in "That Buffalo Hair Fedora," a stunning poem that transforms a story of grief into one of survivance for animal and Native American spirit. Paisley Rekdal writes, "I learned to see the elegy as a form of positive communal remembrance. It's not really a poem of grief so much as a poem of endurance, a restatement of communal values and commitments."

Emotions can be complex. Love can be tinged with sorrow. Or with anger. Grief tinged with mercy can become pity. Poetry seeks out the complexity of human emotion and holds it up for us to see. Joining us together in our sorrows, poetry reminds us of our shared humanity.

From the Oral Tradition of the Aztec

From Mexico come many legends about the disappearance of Quetzalcoatl, the feathered serpent, a major Mesoamerican deity. These songs and stories are vessels to hold collective grief in a time of devastating cultural change and spiritual disorder. In 1547, not long after the fall of the Aztec capital Mexico-Tenochtitlán to the Spanish, the Franciscan monk Bernardino de Sahagún recorded accounts from Aztec oral tradition of Quetzalcoatl's exile, translating the stories from Nahuatl into Spanish. The English version here is translated by Jerome Rothenberg in his influential anthology *Technicians of the Sacred*.

The figure of Quetzalcoatl goes back well over a thousand years, and the meanings attached to the deity have changed over the centuries. Early on he was a creation figure associated with rain and crops, but by the time of the Spanish Conquest, he had broader associations as patron god of the Aztec priesthood, a god of learning and writing. In exile, the feathered serpent must endure a dark journey, and then it reemerges as eternal light, the spiritual order restored. The mythic creature carries the people's burden. What they have suffered may then begin to move toward healing.

THE FLIGHT OF QUETZALCOATL

from the Nahuatl

It ended on the beach
It ended with a hulk of serpents formed into a boat
& when he's made it, sat in it & sailed away
A boat that glided on those burning waters, no one knowing when
    he reached the country of Red Daylight
It ended on the rim of some great sea
It ended with his face reflected in the mirror of its waves
The beauty of his face returned to him
& he was dressed in garments like the sun
It ended with a bonfire on the beach where he would hurl himself
& burn, his ashes rising & the cries of birds
It ended with the linnet, with the birds of turquoise color, birds
    the colors of wild sunflowers, red & blue birds
It ended with the birds of yellow feathers in a riot of bright gold
Circling till the fire had died out
Circling while his heart rose through the sky
It ended with his heart transformed into a star
It ended with the morning star with dawn & evening
It ended with his journey to Death's Kingdom with seven days of darkness
With his body changed to light
A star that burns forever in that sky

A. E. Stallings

A LAMENT FOR THE DEAD PETS OF OUR CHILDHOOD

Even now I dream of rabbits murdered
By loose dogs in the dark, the saved-up voice
Spilt on that last terror, or the springtime
Of lost baby rabbits, grey and blind
As moles, that slipped from birth and from the nest
Into a grey, blind rain, became the mud.
And still I gather up their shapes in dreams,
Those poor, leftover Easter eggs, all grey.

That's how we found out death: the strangled bird
Undone by a toy hung in his cage,
The foundlings that would never last the night,
Be it pigeon, crippled snake, the kitten
Whose very fleas forsook it in the morning
While we nursed a hangover of hope.

After the death of pets, dolls lay too still
And wooden in the cradle, sister, after
We learned death: not hell, no ghosts or angels,
But a cold thing in the image of a warm thing,
Limp as sleep without the twitch of dreams.

SICK FOX

News is not good for foxes on our hillside.
Mange is taking all the newborn kits.
And out for a walk around the neighborhood,
late afternoon, late spring, sky muddy gray—
I saw a grown fox lurch from a laurel thicket
and waver in the middle of the road
that slopes down half a mile to the highway.
I watched her—was she a she?—stagger, stop,
chew at a bald spot on her patchy fur,
fold her legs up oddly, one by one,
and sink down near the white dividing line.
It must have been the illness I was looking at.

She lifted up her head when I came closer
and put it down again. The news is not good.
It must have been that, that I was looking at.
And grief. I was looking at grief.

THE MOTHER

> "The mother octopus lives in the cave for up to seven months
> as the curtain of eggs develops. . . . She doesn't eat during
> this time and usually dies shortly after the young hatch."
>
> —montereybayaquarium.org

It's a slow, steady fade
for her, as her babies
swell into bright being.
The starve. The surrender.
She readies herself for
the guard, prepared to
become ghost for the
sake of her small
selves. She knows
exactly how this will
end. She turns whiter
and whiter until they
are ready and they are
ready and they are
ready. (There are so
many of them and
only one of her.) The
word for her tentacles,
curled around her
young, is a *clutch.*
The length of time in
which she weathers
her watch: a brooding.

Imagine her, perched,
pale and love-long,
in some dark shelf,
knowing she will
never meet what
she has made, and
making, making anyway.
Quiet and final, she
welcomes the empty
with so many many
open arms.

THE LAST SAFE HABITAT

for the Kauaʻi ʻŌʻō, whose song was last heard in 1987

I don't want our daughter to know
that Hawaiʻi is the bird extinction capital
of the world. I don't want her to walk
around the island feeling haunted
by tree roots buried under concrete.
I don't want her to fear the invasive
predators who slither, pounce,
bite, swallow, disease, and multiply.
I don't want her to see paintings
and photographs of birds she'll never
witness in the wild. I don't want her to
imagine their bones in dark museum
drawers. I don't want her to hear
their voice recordings on the internet.
I don't want her to memorize and recite
the names of 77 lost species and subspecies.
I don't want her to draw a timeline
with the years each was "first collected"
and "last sighted." I don't want her to learn
about the Kauaʻi ʻŌʻō, who was observed
atop a flowering ʻŌhiʻa tree, calling
for a mate, day after day, season after
season, because he didn't know he was
the last of his kind—

until one day, he disappeared,
forever, into a nest of avian silence.
I don't want our daughter to calculate
how many miles of fencing is needed
to protect the endangered birds
that remain. I don't want her to realize
the most serious causes of extinction
can't be fenced out. I want to convince her
that extinction is not the end. I want
to convince her that extinction is
just a migration to the last safe habitat
on earth. I want to convince her
that our winged relatives have arrived
safely to their destination: a wondrous
island with a climate we can never
change, and a rainforest fertile
with seeds and song.

W. S. Merwin

FOR A COMING EXTINCTION

Gray whale
Now that we are sending you to The End
That great god
Tell him
That we who follow you invented forgiveness
And forgive nothing

I write as though you could understand
And I could say it
One must always pretend something
Among the dying
When you have left the seas nodding on their stalks
Empty of you
Tell him that we were made
On another day

The bewilderment will diminish like an echo
Winding along your inner mountains
Unheard by us
And find its way out
Leaving behind it the future
Dead
And ours

When you will not see again
The whale calves trying the light
Consider what you will find in the black garden
And its court
The sea cows the Great Auks the gorillas
The irreplaceable hosts ranged countless
And fore-ordaining as stars
Our sacrifices

Join your word to theirs
Tell him
That it is we who are important

MR. CASS AND THE CRUSTACEANS

Whales the color of milk have washed ashore
in Germany, their stomachs clogged full
of plastic and car parts. Imagine the splendor
of a creature as big as half a football field—

the magnificence of the largest brain
of any animal—modern or extinct. I have
been trying to locate my fourth grade
science teacher for years. Mr. Cass, who

gave us each a crawfish he found just past
the suburbs of Phoenix, before strip malls
licked every good desert with cold blast
of Freon and glass. Mr. Cass who played

soccer with us at recess, who let me check
on my wily, snappy crawfish in the plastic
blue pool before class started so I could place
my face to the surface of the water and see

if it still skittered alive. I hate to admit
how much this meant to me, the only brown girl
in the classroom. How I wish I could tell Mr. Cass
how I've never stopped checking the waters—

the ponds, the lakes, the sea. And I worry
that I've yet to see a sperm whale, except when
they beach themselves in coves. How many songs
must we hear from the sun-bleached bones

of a seabird or whale? If there were anyone on earth
who would know this, Mr. Cass, it's you—how even
bottle caps found inside a baby albatross corpse
can make a tiny ribcage whistle when the ocean wind

blows through it just right—I know wherever you are,
you'd weep if you heard this sad music. I think
how you first taught us kids to listen to water,
and I'm grateful for each story in its song.

PITY THE SWINE ITS SUCCULENCE

Pig, pig, repellent chop, rutting hock,
sow of sorrows, hated by half
the known world, cut down in your prime
by the rest. You are despised
whether eaten or not. Filthy, fat,
enticing as the apple in your mouth.

Cows when uneaten are revered.
A clover path lay before them, as they
in dim-eyed indifference munch
their cud. For those who do partake,
bovines are admired for their marbling
fat—

and no one yells DIRTY CHICKEN—
though the chicken
pushes its beak through small clods
of its own shit to find an undigested seed.

So why detest the hog in its pen?

Can we deny the perfume
of its renderings waking us
from a dream of fields.
Or how its ampleness sustains
us in godlike manifestations,
taking on whatever we need it to be;
holiday ham, enemy of nations.

Pity the swine its succulence,
the delectable fat that will not be
denied, tempting us into gluttony,
into shame. The sweet pink flesh
hidden as desire and its object is
so often hidden, just below the bristle.

Robert Wrigley

ELK

His hindquarters must have fallen through
the ice, and he could not pull himself back out
and the incoming colder weather
refroze the hole around him and he died,
sinking some, only his broad horns
holding his head and neck above the surface.
Soon he must have been discovered by coyotes,
who ate all they could. His face, that is,
the soft, perhaps just frozen, cheeks and muzzle,
his tongue, which would have protruded
from his open dying mouth, the eyes,
then the opening of the throat, the coyotes'
prints visible only in the sheen of blood
around the snowless black surface of the lake.
Such cold this early in the winter, autumn really,
still early December, has surprised us all.
Since snow is at last forecast this afternoon,
I have come to skate, half a mile from shore
when I see him, or see what's left,
and reconstruct the narrative of his demise.
The coyotes ignored his spraddled forelegs,
hoof prints still born down against the pull
of his back half. A six-point bull elk,
some abrasions on the surface of the ice
where the horns thrashed but held him.
A half-mile skate back to where I hung my boots
from a limb, a hundred yard walk from there
to the truck, in which I keep a bow saw,

which I could use to remove a wedge of pate
with the perfect rack, but I choose not to.
Something in the weariness of the bones
of his jaw, also the snow just now beginning.
Given the altitude here, he'll be completely covered
in a month, and at break-up, late March
or early April, he will sink as he did not
yesterday or the day before, and the bones
and the horns of him will settle to the bottom.
Although the coyotes may be back tonight,
to dig their way from the horns' stumps
for the ears, which I notice are still whole and upright,
the left one turned slightly farther left,
as though, with the last of his miraculous
senses, he heard them coming over the ice.

THAT BUFFALO HAIR FEDORA

i.
Summer dreads on a two-ton buffalo
viewed through the zoom lens of my Canon—
not the sleek and groomed, not the enviable
cooler than trench poet locs
on Quincy Troupe, nor the tough mama
you could lose dimes and pennies in there
hair of rasta soccer coach Michelle.
No, these are the *don't mess with me*
I've got Yellowstone grasslands in my fur dreads,
the *oh yes! you better take your pictures*
from the safety of your van's skylight perch dreads,
and the *I make thunder with my hooves* dreads.

ii.
That buffalo-hair fedora on a long lean Comanche—
prairie strands that withstood snow and wind, gathered
groomed into this dashing caramel-colored topper.
A hat of history sits now upon dark braids. Waist-length,
this hair like bison survival a sublime defiance.

iii.

A colonial greed older than prairie hills
a destiny made manifest in slaughter
of grazing bison, in military-style schools
where our children were herded into classrooms
taught with small tortures to recover
from their primitive and ungodly lifestyles,
where chongos and squash blossom whorls
braids and roached hair dropped heavy to the floor
landed and piled there like gut-shot buffalo.

iv.

That bull fresh from mud wallowing
that massive herbivore has fed on leaves
and twigs, bark, berries, and grasses,
he wears like a crown the evidence of contact
with willow, ash, and especially blackberry.
That wild oxen legendary for head-butting
in rut, legendary too for spring shedding,
will supply soft down we spin and weave,
coarse strands we braid and twist into rope.

v.

Today that sleek buffalo hair fedora, yesterday
tufts of insulation for winter moccasins,
stuffing for dolls and balls,
thread, horse halters, and brushes for paint,
rugs, blankets, girdles, and garters—
yes, buffalo hair sashes, bags,
and earrings, harnesses and hair extensions:
then and now, these buffalo hair dreadlocks
touched, marked by sweet prairie earth.

vi.

Count then the myriad uses of a hairy clump
the numbers of squandered bison or Native bodies
the things mystical we try to tame,
the holy oldness of copper, of order, of name
these micro centimeters between beauty and loss:
that solemn, that survivance—this sweet smooth
this coming from prairie centuries
this buffalo hair fedora.

SMOKEY

The bear coughs the bristlecone smoke like the rest of us,
but isn't allowed into the visitors' center for AC and free Kool-Aid.
No one said it was easy being an icon, a t-shirt, an ad campaign.
And what can I learn from the bear? He wears a GPS ear tag
and I an iPhone as I sit alone for two days in smoky Yosemite,
an abandoned husband with a burning heart. Half Dome
is more Beijing smog than Ansel Adams gelatin print wilderness.
Across the Sierras the Smokey signs feel useless. Endless helicopters
drop dispersant. The bear and I see extinction out of the corners
of our eyes. The annual fires roaring across the West are extinction
and administration's selling off public lands is extinction,
the last grizzly in the Sierras was once extinction, the cougar
crossing the highway a protest of extinction. The story ends
with the real Smokey sleeping out his days in D.C.'s National Zoo,
dreaming of sagebrush while retirees eat wieners and point.
A boy grows up, his head dreaming on a teddy bear. Without realizing it,
his life is a shrine to bears. Bears in Alaska. Bears in Hokkaido.
Bears in the Andes. Bears in Quebec. Bears that don't promise
self-actualization or a good 401K or freedom from cancer.
Bears that knock around the soul without permission.
Bears that ruin a marriage. The boy becomes a man who wants
to love women, but they will never smell like bears. People are people
but bears are a secret howling ladder to a world of smoky caves.
Even as I try not to think about bears, Smokey ambles slowly away,
his fur wet with my dreams. I have no right to bring him back to life.

Elizabeth Bradfield

THE VOICE OF THE MANATEE

The voice of the manatee is shrill,
harsh as a rusted pennywhistle.
This only increases my pity, my
sad head shaking at the propeller cutwork

lathed across its muddy hide because
although its screeches rise
toward the whine of machines, it can't
hear the Evinrude, all cavitation and churn

speeding the bungalow-lined and dredged
canals of Cocoa Beach. It doesn't flinch
at kids, loud with riffs of jibe and cheer,
tossing Snackables into the mangrove roots.

The pitch of harm has been recalibrated,
and the manatee's ear isn't tuned. To it,
danger sounds like distant rumble:
a car door slams two blocks away and the manatee

lazing by the culvert, suckling
the sweet water of a garden hose
left running, twitches its bulk
and slowly begins to flee.

Above, another space shuttle
flares toward space. Below,
turtlegrass grows through old tires.
Warm water flows from the power plant.

Here is what it senses: the grass is sweet,
the canal's currents slow.
A ways off, another manatee skrills:
sweet grass, still waters, warmth.

COMPANIONSHIP

Among the gifts that come to us from animals is their companionship. I could have collected an entire anthology about our lovable—and sometimes vexing—pets. Dogs and cats abound in poetry. In our social isolation during the COVID-19 pandemic, more than 23 million American households adopted a pet, according to the American Society for the Prevention of Cruelty to Animals. Happily, I am among them and have come to learn anew how comforting and interesting it is to live with an animal, a fellow perceiver in the wonder of living.

One evening when my pup was still quite small, we stood quietly in the backyard together. I noticed that she was staring up at the night sky. Staring and staring. I followed her gaze and saw what she had seen. She had no words to describe the full moon. But her attention drew my gaze to see it. I treasure such shared moments among our daily rituals. I start and end my day in conversation with an animal companion, and how much richer my days have become.

Companionship with animals extends well beyond our domestic critters. These poems speak to a wide range of experience. Ever Jones hears the way "coyote howl softens the air into aria," suggesting the companionship of wild song. Michael Collier describes people in a restaurant leaving their tables and crowding together at the window to see javelinas—"archaic creatures . . . with cobalt eyes"—passing in the desert. We hear of a man who must euthanize his old mare, embracing the animal in a final gesture of tender companionship. A woman who rears 321 frogs. And a reflection on a lifelong relationship with owls, reminding us of the companionship between children and imaginary animals.

When it comes to the power of animal companionship, sometimes all a person needs is to be in the presence of wild creatures—for Wendell Berry, the wood drake or great heron—in order to "rest in the grace of the world."

From the Japanese Haiku Tradition

In the poetry traditions of Japan and China, the landscape is a source of inspiration, giving order to a chaotic universe. Mountains and rivers are central images, as are the seasons and their cyclical patterns. Yosa Buson (1716–1784) was an esteemed Japanese painter and haiku poet of the Edo Period. He was the son of a wealthy farmer, by some accounts, and first studied acting and painting. He then spent 10 years as a wandering poet, in the tradition of the haiku master Basho, earning his living as an artist. He settled in Kyoto and turned his creative attention to poetry.

Haiku, in addition to its formal constraints, focuses on time and place, the seasons of the year, and the cyclical patterns in nature. The frog shows up in many haikus as a symbol of return. Indeed, the Japanese word for frog, *kaeru*, is also the word for "return." The frog is associated with spring and summer, the time of renewal and thriving in nature. It is seen as an omamori, a charm against bad luck.

Buson's haiku is translated by renowned poet, translator, and essayist Robert Hass. We live in an age of attention deficit, when every quiet moment is filled by engaging with cyber distractions. Buson's attention is keen to what surrounds him, so keen that his senses blur, and, in a moment of synesthesia, he "sees" the croaking of frogs and "listens" to the moon. It is a time of fruition, Heaven and Earth in balance.

LISTENING TO THE MOON

from the Japanese text by Yosa Buson

Listening to the moon,
gazing at the croaking of frogs
in a field of ripe rice.

Christopher Smart

from JUBILATE AGNO

For I will consider my Cat Jeoffry.

For he is the servant of the Living God duly and daily serving him.

For at the first glance of the glory of God in the East he worships in his way.

For this is done by wreathing his body seven times round with elegant quickness.

For then he leaps up to catch the musk, which is the blessing of God upon his prayer.

For he rolls upon prank to work it in.

For having done duty and received blessing he begins to consider himself.

For this he performs in ten degrees.

For first he looks upon his forepaws to see if they are clean.

For secondly he kicks up behind to clear away there.

For thirdly he works it upon stretch with the forepaws extended.

For fourthly he sharpens his paws by wood.

For fifthly he washes himself.

For sixthly he rolls upon wash.

For seventhly he fleas himself, that he may not be interrupted upon the beat.

For eighthly he rubs himself against a post.

For ninthly he looks up for his instructions.

For tenthly he goes in quest of food.

For having consider'd God and himself he will consider his neighbour.

For if he meets another cat he will kiss her in kindness.

For when he takes his prey he plays with it to give it a chance.

For one mouse in seven escapes by his dallying.

For when his day's work is done his business more properly begins.

For he keeps the Lord's watch in the night against the adversary.

For he counteracts the powers of darkness by his electrical skin and glaring eyes.

For he counteracts the Devil, who is death, by brisking about the life.

For in his morning orisons he loves the sun and the sun loves him.

For he is of the tribe of Tiger.

For the Cherub Cat is a term of the Angel Tiger.

For he has the subtlety and hissing of a serpent, which in goodness he suppresses.

For he will not do destruction, if he is well-fed, neither will he spit without provocation.

For he purrs in thankfulness, when God tells him he's a good Cat.

For he is an instrument for the children to learn benevolence upon.

For every house is incomplete without him and a blessing is lacking in the spirit.

YOKO

All today I lie in the bottom of the wardrobe
feeling low but sometimes getting up
to moodily lumber across rooms
and lap from the toilet bowl, it is so sultry
and then I hear the noise of firecrackers again
all New York is jaggedy with firecrackers today
and I go back to the wardrobe gloomy
trying to void my mind of them.
I am confused, I feel loose and unfitted.

At last deep in the stairwell I hear a tread,
it is him, my leader, my love.
I run to the door and listen to his approach.
Now I can smell him, what a good man he is,
I love it when he has the sweat of work on him,
as he enters I yodel with happiness,
I throw my body up against his, I try to lick his lips,
I care about him more than anything.

After we eat we go for a walk to the piers.
I leap into the standing warmth, I plunge into
the combination of old and new smells.
Here on a garbage can at the bottom, so interesting,
what sister or brother I wonder left this message I sniff.
I too piss there, and go on.
Here a hydrant there a pole
here's a smell I left yesterday, well that's disappointing
but I piss there anyway, and go on.

I investigate so much that in the end
it is for form's sake only, only a drop comes out.

I investigate tar and rotten sandwiches, everything, and go on.

And here a dried old turd, so interesting
so old, so dry, yet so subtle and mellow.
I can place it finely, I really appreciate it,
a gold distant smell like packed autumn leaves in winter
reminding me how what is rich and fierce when excreted
becomes weathered and mild
                    but always interesting
and reminding me of what I have to do.

My leader looks on and expresses his approval.

I sniff it well and later I sniff the air well
a wind is meeting us after the close July day
rain is getting near too but first the wind.
Joy, joy,
being outside with you, active, investigating it all,
with bowels emptied, feeling your approval
and then running on, the big fleet Yoko,
my body in its excellent black coat never lets me down,
returning to you (as I always will, you know that)
and now
        filling myself out with myself, no longer confused,
my panting pushing apart my black lips, but unmoving,
I stand with you braced against the wind.

TWO KEROSENE LANTERNS

The cat walks the narrow shelf beneath the window
where many delicate things are arranged—polished ammonites,
a dried starfish, three turtle netsuke,
a few curls of birch bark, two long-unused kerosene lanterns.

As if on their own, two hands fly up to cover the person's face,
to cover the eyes already closed.

The crash, as it must, arrives.

The hands lower slowly.
The cat sits on the floor in the room's middle, calmly licking one paw.

The law of cats is simple: one arrangement becomes another.

People are strange.

THE ART OF THE DOG

In Mary Cassatt's *Little Blue Armchair*,
it's not the child I look at but the Norwich terrier,
twin to mine, curled up on another armchair.
And in Picasso's *Boy with Dog*, I want
to enter the famous Blue Period to pat it.

There are dogs in the cave paintings in France,
and the hounds in the Bayeaux Tapestry
are stitched into the scene by hand, chasing
their embroidered prey right into art history.

It's said that dogs in paintings
domesticate the scene or symbolize love,
that even a still life of flowers and fruit
may have a poodle or dachshund
hidden under the table.

Is a painted dog different
from a dog in a poem—from a dog,
like mine for instance, who follows
me from stanza to stanza as if I'm going
to throw a pencil for him to retrieve
instead of the usual ball?

Velasquez's *Maids of Honor* . . .
Madame Renoir with a Dog . . . Van Eyck's
marriage scene, complete with terrier . . . .
At night the museums echo
with the unleashed sound of barking.

Jose Hernandez Diaz

TECOLOTE

The Mexican word for owl is tecolote, from the Nahuatl: tecolotl.
I think it sounds beautiful in both languages: both of my origins.

My favorite bird is the tecolote. The way it sits in the tree:
Wise insomniac, alone. Only company is rain. At night, it comes alive:

A little moon. A myth. A continent of leaves. At midnight: the tecolote
Transforms into a jaguar, into a python, into a dragon.

When I was younger, my mom used to tell me I was like
A tecolote because I would stay up late to watch Letterman or

Conan O'Brien. Then, as a teenager, I was a tecolote because I would
Go out late with friends and party. Now, at thirty-five, I'm getting

A tattoo of a tecolote on my forearm. Reminder of my childhood,
My ancestry, the night. Gracias, tecolote: protector of the moon and sky.

TURKEYS, BUCKS AND BULLS

it was for approval. to show the woman who
came from the Jicarilla hills—I too could skin a buck
it was for the elk bugles, turkey calls, and deer tracks
that would be my son's first language

it was so the sun had a companion at his rise
we would ride out together, waking the spruce
nudging the dirt with our toes, war cries, early morning lies

it was for buckshot sightings, crouching, breathe, blood, breathe
blessings given, blessings taken, a labor prayer
it was for the speed of skinning
the skill, the sense of some ancestral assurance
here was the leather, here was the sinew, here was the shed
I for myself
here was the fluff, here was the fan, here were the feathers
I shot for you
it was so we could chew the sap
it was for the viscera, the falcon mothers, vulture young
it was for the numb knuckles
it was for the death smell, the love smell
it was so the sun could nod every morning, but the Jicarilla
        woman never would

DRAWL AND HUM

Three hundred twenty is the number
        of frogs I've raised
and released during the pandemic.
        Yes, I'm trying to impress you,
but I don't count the dead.
        The ones the hunter drove over.
The ones that dried up
        with the puddle they came from.
The ones eaten by their siblings
        because I filled my casserole dishes
with too many. Yes, clouds drag
        their feet, clothes sour
on the line, and tomatoes bust open
        in the garden. Every day
drawls and hums this song
        that won't end.
But then, the 321st froglet
        climbs out, tail still swishing,
certain this world
        is as humid as the last.
Ready to join the choir.

Boars gleaning through cities at night

caught on CCTV cameras
are eerie one-dimensional
shadows, emerging,
occupying, then passing
through the emptiness
of their own obscurity.
Sometimes they'll appear
more boldly in herds,
such as those marauding
a Palermo cemetery
or in Rome
in broad daylight, surrounding
a woman carrying groceries.

                    *

Closer to home but farther
in the past . . . I featured
a *javelina* in a poem
but was told by an older poet
the word didn't exist
and it didn't in the venerable
out-of-date dictionary
used to prove the point,
but all I had to do was close
my eyes to see the pair, nosing
the ground outside Scordato's,
1980, west of Tucson,

at the edge of the great
saguaro forest.

*

Had I known a *javelina*
is not a boar,
not even a pig, although
it looks like both
I might have asked the poet
to look up *peccary*,
but how would I have done that
without impertinence?
Saguaros are not trees.
Who would insist they are?
And yet outside Scordato's
in the dark, an incontrovertible
forest of them stood, while
two *javelinas* grazed.

*

Those of us nearest the windows
left our tables and soon others,
from across the room, crowded
to peer into the night,
and with some difficulty
discerned in the layers
of shadowy reflections
shapes that seemed to occupy
a benthic realm,
archaic creatures, encroaching,

born of the deep, palpable,
with cobalt eyes
and known to us
as their name.

from NIGHTSONG

Coyote howl softens the air into aria
      & an apple thumps the ground with nightsong
         we don't know why the leaf suddenly shivers
         or which paw snapped the blackened stick
     but we stay in their echoes until the wound
passes like a sieve of humid air
     i am loved here
         in the moon's half-phase
            you shining the stars for me
         making the galaxy just another walk to the sink
     in this new light an owl settles on the ledge beyond sight
            giving me a silence far more salient than any word

A SONNET AT THE EDGE OF THE REEF

the Waikīkī Aquarium

We dip our hands into the outdoor reef exhibit
and touch sea cucumber and red urchin
as butterflyfish swim by. A docent explains:
once a year, after the full moon, when tides swell
to a certain height, and saltwater reaches the perfect
temperature, only then will the ocean cue coral
polyps to spawn, in synchrony, a galaxy of gametes,
which dances to the surface, fertilizes, opens,
forms larvae, roots to seafloor, and grows, generation
upon generation. At home, we read a children's
book, *The Great Barrier Reef*, to our daughter
snuggling between us in bed. We don't mention
corals bleaching, reared in labs, or frozen.
And isn't our silence, too, a kind of shelter?

WEAKNESS

Old mare whose eyes
are like cracked marbles,
drools blood in her mash,
shivers in her jute blanket.

My father hates weakness worse than hail;
in the morning
    without haste
he will shoot her in the ear, once,
shovel her under in the north pasture.

Tonight
    leaving the stables,
he stands his lantern on an overturned water pail,
turns,
    cursing her for a bad bargain,
and spreads his coat
carefully over her sick shoulders.

THE PEACE OF WILD THINGS

When despair for the world grows in me
and I wake in the night at the least sound
in fear of what my life and my children's lives may be,
I go and lie down where the wood drake
rests in his beauty on the water, and the great heron feeds.
I come into the peace of wild things
who do not tax their lives with forethought
of grief. I come into the presence of still water.
And I feel above me the day-blind stars
waiting with their light. For a time
I rest in the grace of the world, and am free.

FEAR AND VULNERABILITY

Fear is a survival mechanism. It warns us of a threat. The mind perceives a danger, and the brain triggers the body to protect itself. The nervous system goes on high alert, stress hormones flow, breath quickens, blood pumps into limbs preparing for fight or flight. Some of us like to practice fear and the feeling of vulnerability by watching horror films or by skydiving. Perhaps it helps to strengthen us for the times when we face an actual threat. I like to watch murder mysteries: A violence is committed, and the story ends with a crime solved. In real life, violence does not play out so neatly.

We live in violent times: wars, mass murder, racial violence, violence against women, extinctions, extreme and devastating weather events. Poems acknowledge the reality of our fears and vulnerability. They may, for a moment, take the pressure off. The way we see animals depends very much on the lens, cultural and personal, through which we see them. What images might arise when a Black man in America sees a white-headed bird? Poems teach us to see through the eyes of the vulnerable other, to acknowledge our human capacity for violence and the price it exacts on our collective well-being. As creatures aware of our mortality, we understand what it is to be vulnerable and to fear. Perhaps poems help us to manage our fears and have empathy for others. We find comfort in sharing our stories.

Jane Hirshfield writes, "Poems, for me, are written because there is some fracture that needs addressing. You write because something is off-kilter, bewildering, devastating." Poems imagine their way into the animal experience of fear and vulnerability. What might it feel like to be a tiny rabbit in fear of a predator? Or caught in a wildfire? Fear and vulnerability heighten awareness. Fear helps keep us safe. Understanding the vulnerability of another—even, say, a little mammoth frozen in ice for 40 thousand years—can bring out the tenderness in us. And fear can also be used to exert power and control over others.

From the Hymns of Ancient Sumeria

Enheduana, high priestess and royal princess in the ancient city of Ur, now southern Iraq, may be the first author of written literature. She lived about 2300 BCE. Her songs were written in Sumerian and etched into clay tablets. Because clay is vulnerable to erosion and breakage, the poems as we know them have gaps, indicated by dots in the excerpts below.

Translator Sophus Helle asks, "What would the history of Western literature look like if it began not with Homer and his war-hungry heroes but with a woman from ancient Iraq who sang her hymns to the goddess of chaos and change?" Enheduana's "Hymns to Inana" addresses the deity of war, sex, change, and destruction. The hymns celebrate the awesome power of Inana and look to the animal world for images of ferocity, employing fear to secure the goddess's power. "Inana, hawk of the gods, shreds up the sheepfold."

from HYMNS TO INANA

from the Sumerian text by Enheduana

Sitting on leashed
lions, Inana rips
apart those who
feel no fear of her.
Like a leopard of
the mountains, she
bursts onto the road
. . . .

. . . .

Queen, huge aurochs!
Fierce in her might,
no one turns to fight
her . . . .

Emily Dickinson

A NARROW FELLOW IN THE GRASS

A narrow Fellow in the Grass
Occasionally rides—
You may have met him? Did you not
His notice instant is—

The Grass divides as with a Comb,
A spotted Shaft is seen,
And then it closes at your Feet
And opens further on—

He likes a Boggy Acre—
A Floor too cool for Corn—
But when a Boy and Barefoot
I more than once at Noon

Have passed I thought a Whip Lash
Unbraiding in the Sun
When stooping to secure it
It wrinkled And was gone—

Several of Nature's People
I know, and they know me
I feel for them a transport
Of Cordiality

But never met this Fellow
Attended or alone
Without a tighter Breathing
And Zero at the Bone.

NEARLY EVERY INVADING ARMY BROUGHT PIGS WITH THEM TO FEED THEIR SOLDIERS

they reproduce so quick generations could be eaten during a single siege.

adaptable they followed, devouring towns and forests, so soldiers ate

the worlds they invaded. even after illness swept through the men like wind

through a grain silo, the pigs they left behind, killing the hillside, remain.

BLACK FLAMINGO

Learned today that flamingoes can live up to seventy years.
I gasped at the fact, thinking about a bird, pink and slender

and older than my parents, out there somewhere preening
its coat of feathers, or sifting through a lake of food,

a flock of them flying southeast, their bodies against the sky
like a postcard.

Meanwhile, several states from here, another Black twenty-something
who could've been me, but wasn't for no reason other than chance,

was killed in his sleep,
his name against the TV like a Wednesday.

What does it mean when I wish us all the lives of birds?
Don't we deserve a vibrant life? A colorful life?

A life where we can strut into the water
wearing our years like a gown?

RABBITS AND FIRE

Everything's been said
But one last thing about the desert,
And it's awful: During brush fires in the Sonoran desert,
Brush fires that happen before the monsoon and in the great,
Deep, wide, and smothering heat of the hottest months,
The longest months,
The hypnotic, immeasurable lulls of August and July—
During these summer fires, jackrabbits—
Jackrabbits and everything else
That lives in the brush of the rolling hills,
But jackrabbits especially—
Jackrabbits can get caught in the flames,
No matter how fast and big and strong and sleek they are.
And when they're caught,
Cornered in and against the thick
Trunks and thin spines of the cactus,
When they can't back up any more,
When they can't move, the flame—
It touches them,
And their fur catches fire.
Of course, they run away from the flame,
Finding movement even when there is none to be found,
Jumping big and high over the wave of fire, or backing
Even harder through the impenetrable
Tangle of hardened saguaro
And prickly pear and cholla and barrel,
But whichever way they find,
What happens is what happens: They catch fire

And then bring the fire with them when they run.
They don't know they're on fire at first,
Running so fast as to make the fire
Shoot like rocket engines and smoke behind them,
But then the rabbits tire
And the fire catches up,
Stuck onto them like the needles of the cactus,
Which at first must be what they think they feel on their skins.
They've felt this before, every rabbit.
But this time the feeling keeps on.
And of course, they ignite the brush and dried weeds
All over again, making more fire, all around them.
I'm sorry for the rabbits.
And I'm sorry for us
To know this.

DRIVING TO SANTA FE

Quick swim up
through the headlights: gold eye
a startle in black: green swift glance
raking mine. A full second
we held each other, gone.
Gone. And how did I know
what to call it? *Lynx*, the only possible
reply though I'd never seen one. The car
filling with it: moonlight,
piñon: a cat's acrid smell
of terror. How quickly the gray body
fled, swerving to avoid
my light. And how often
that sight returns to me, shames me
to know how much more this fragment
matters. More than the broad back
of a man I loved. More than the image
of my friend, cancer-struck, curled
by her toilet. More than my regret
for the child I did not have which I thought
once would pierce me, utterly. Nothing
beside that dense muscle, faint gold guard hairs
stirring the dark. And if I keep
these scraps of it, what did it keep of me?

A flight, a thunder. A shield of light
dropped before the eyes, pinned
inside that magnificent skull only time
would release. Split back, fade
and reveal. Wind
would open him. Sun would turn him
commonplace: a knot of flies, a ribcage
of shredded tendon, wasp-nest
fragile. The treasure of him, like anything,
gone. Even now, I thumb that face
like a coin I cannot spend. If something in me
ever lived, it lived in him, fishing the cold
trout-thick streams, waking to snow, dying
when he died, which is a comfort.
I must say this. Otherwise, I myself
do not exist. It looked at me
a moment. A flash of green, of gold
and white. Then the dark came down again
between us. Once, I was afraid
of being changed. Now that is finished.
The lynx has me in its eye.
I am already diminished.

THE MINKS

In the backyard of our house on Norwood,
there were five hundred steel cages lined up,
each with a wooden box
roofed with tar paper;
inside, two stories, with straw
for a bed. Sometimes the minks would pace
back and forth wildly, looking for a way out;
or else they'd hide in their wooden houses, even when
we'd put the offering of raw horse meat on their trays, as if
they knew they were beautiful
and wanted to deprive us.
In spring the placid kits
drank with glazed eyes.
Sometimes the mothers would go mad
and snap their necks.
My uncle would lift the roof like a god
who might lift our roof, look down on us
and take us out to safety.
Sometimes one would escape.
He would go down on his hands and knees,
aiming a flashlight like
a bullet of light, hoping to catch
the orange gold of its eyes.
He wore huge boots, gloves
so thick their little teeth couldn't bite through.
"They're wild," he'd say. "Never trust them."

Each afternoon when I put the scoop of raw meat rich
with eggs and vitamins on their trays,
I'd call to each a greeting.
Their small thin faces would follow as if slightly curious.
In fall they went out in a van, returning
sorted, matched, their skins hanging down on huge metal
hangers, pinned by their mouths.
My uncle would take them out when company came
and drape them over his arm—the sweetest cargo.
He'd blow down the pelts softly
and the hairs would part for his breath
and show the shining underlife which, like
the shining of the soul, gives us each
character and beauty.

Oleh Lysheha
translated from the Ukrainian by Virlana Tkacz & Wanda Phipps

RABBIT

I recognize the beaten path
And the worn out roadside—
Where the cattle were driven,
Before there were vans—
My pliable, great ears
Were filled to the brim with metal rattling. .
Who can shout into them now,
Where is my home on the edge of the forest,
That was fenced off with hazel and wild cherry twigs. .
Maybe, I did not run the right way? . .
Maybe, I wanted too much—to grow bigger.
Jump higher?—be clean, always fit—
When did this cast iron darkness pour into me and how?
It seems, all my lightness
Thickened into one great immovable mass,
A hard lump of earth,
On the one hand like
A pregnant female rabbit with drooping lids
The night before giving birth,
On the other like a slippery baby rabbit
On its first night when it's about to crawl
Away from the breast into an uncaring world. .
Its poor undeveloped ears. . what noise will they hear
A little later, after a jump or two,
Or a couple of dozen river crossings. .
Or after outrunning hundreds of dogs?. .

Hawk, do you hear me—I am not a rabbit!
I am not a rabbit!—out in the middle of a field. .
That's just a messy pile of red clover?!.

THE EMMY GOES TO THE SEAGULL, FLYING OFF WITH THE HOT WING . . . IN FRONT OF THE CHICKEN SPOT?

And I was like,
but ain't that shit cannibalism?
Ain't that your cousin in some retrospect?

I should be more empathetic to hot wing homie,
flying off with fam drenched in Frank's Red Hot cloaked all over its claws.
I might be witnessing a long-distance funeral;
I recognize that we need physical evidence in order to personalize our grief.

I walk into Whole Foods and think
damn,
somebody's house
was ripped out of the ground
to make room for this poultry section.
Government done stole somebody's livelihood,
then gave them a job,
as a cashier,
in the store
of the home
they ripped them from.

Maybe that seagull was onto its way to a memorial.
Maybe he knows, and doesn't plan to eat cousin Hector in Red Hot.
Maybe Hot Wing Homie has a shrine on the corner of a Wing Stop
where he's actively protesting Lemon Peppers and we can't hear him
because the crunch from crispy skins drowns him out.

I am standing in front of a Telco in the neighborhood that raised me
but can no longer afford.
A Chinese Buffet, into a Starbucks.
The wedding boutique, is a Taco Bell.
I hear a Jamaican woman in the distance proclaim to a customer
"We ran out of oxtail,"
and I pray for more of those grievances.

As I turn the corner,
I peep Hot Wing Homie hiding behind a 2010 Range Rover,
piercing his claws into his cousin.
Tearin' that wing up,
Frank's Red Hot smeared across the beak and I say,
Damn, sometimes it be cannibalism.

CARNIVORE

> "This is my body, which is given
> for you; do this in remembrance
> of me." —Luke 22:19

I slept, and in my sleeping
became the things I loved
and killed. More than twenty
deer. Nearly fifty cows.
Eighty-five hogs
and thirty-one lambs.
Countless rabbits
longing to mate in their dens,
and ninety-three squirrels
searching the treetops
for leafy nests. Sixty-six
of the best tasting ducks, teal
and ring-necked divers,
presented at the feet
by a good dog's jaws,
by a canine persistence
I'm still learning to obey.
I slaver at the sound of geese
flying over the tops of sycamore
in the flood plain. I'm a slave
to the memory of each one
I've plucked and gutted, the many

animals I've butchered and eaten,
so when I rise from the pool
of blood my dreams float in,
the fire sparks with dripping fat,
with the smell of my own
burning flesh consumed
in the body's oven.

Wang Jiaxin
translated from the Chinese by Arthur Sze

ICE ANGLERS

In the reservoir near my house, when winter comes,
you can see some ice anglers,
squatting there in old army overcoats.
From a distance, they look like crows scattered in the snow.
They crouch there as if time has stopped.
They go there just so fish can breathe, under a single ray of light —
the fish swim hesitantly up to the holes.
The ice anglers' ecstasy is to see living creatures
thrash their tails in pain on ice,
until blood seeps from their gills,
staining red the piles of chiseled ice . . .
These are the most frightening sights I can imagine —
I turned away from that embankment;
I tried to think it was just a chance encounter in my stroll.

LITTLE MAMMOTH

Mother's milk in my belly

and a little of her shit, too,
so that I might eat

of the sour-green steppes
that opened endlessly

before me, though not long
after I slid into sunlight

and the grass-world I slid
again into the mudhole,

and screamed, and screaming
sucked clay into my trunk

till I lay on the bottom,
my milk-tusks not even

sprouted, a sweet undercoat
of fat ready for my first winter,

and I am still one month old, and
forty thousand years without my mother.

THE WHITE-HEADED WOODPECKER

Quiet. Given to prying more than pecking, an odd member
of the family, lives only in the high pine forests of western

mountains like the Cascades, where I spent an afternoon
almost a decade ago in Roslyn, Washington looking for what

I could find of Black people who'd migrated from the South
almost a century and a quarter prior. The white-headed

woodpecker doesn't migrate and so is found in its
home range year-round when it can be found. Roslyn,

founded as a coal mining town, drew miners from all over
Europe—as far away as Croatia—across the ocean, with

opportunities. With their hammering and drilling to extract
a living, woodpeckers could be considered arboreal miners.

A habitat, a home range, is where one can feed and house
oneself—meet the requirements of life—and propagate.

In 1888, those miners from many lands all in Roslyn came
together to go on strike against the mine management.

And so, from Southern states, a few hundred Black miners
were recruited with the promise of opportunities in Roslyn,

many with their families in tow, to break the strike. They
faced resentment and armed resistance, left in the dark

until their arrival, unwitting scabs—that healing that happens
after lacerations or abrasions. Things settled down as they do

sometimes, and eventually Blacks and whites entered a union
as equals. Black save for a white face and crown and a sliver

of white on its wings that flares to a crescent when they
spread for flight, the white-headed woodpecker is a study

in contrasts. Males have a patch of red feathers
on the back of their crowns, and I can't help but see blood.

Brian Bartlett

EVERY LION UNTIL NOW

Every lion until now was sun-faced, lacy-maned,
a Leo with beaming eyes and no hint of claws.
A child who first walked ten months ago
learns the word "dark," giving the "d" and the "k"
their full force. Now he says "lion"
with his voice shaking, his lip lowered
in fear, then lion and dark go together.

He sees a beast in the murk below
basement stairs, under the rocking chair
by his costume box, in shadowed
distances of the study. His parents can't say
how the plush creature changed overnight
any more than how the first manticore
stalked through a mind thousands of years back.
Maybe one day the child gazed into a mirror
and found the darkness behind his own teeth;
maybe he began to hear the danger
in his own comical roar. Fear
is more than a taste he doesn't like,
more than a strategy to get his way. Weeks ago
the first slap of ocean waves against his legs
made him whimper and ask to be held.

The father thinks: *The dark needs a body,*
the lion serves the purpose. Some maw
opens and opens and would swallow
all—boy, room, house. When their son runs
to their legs, the parents look into the obscurity

he shows them, and they glimpse again
the breeding cave of their own dread,
a source nothing on earth lights up.

THE LEAST
AMONG US

Charismatic megafauna—dinosaurs and tigers and giraffes—excite the imagination, but none of them would be here without the least among us: microbes, ants, bees, crickets, scorpions. Bugs do the basic work of pollination and decomposition, stirring up the soil and cleaning up everyone's mess with their fastidious appetites. And creatures considered objects of ridicule or annoyance, like the sloth and the squirrel, can be seen for their hidden talents and the way they speak to something within us.

Poems can shift our frame of reference from human-centered to animistic. Or a difficult truth—the violence of racism—can find its way into the smallest vessel, say a cricket, or a tree frog. Or in seeing, really seeing, the cockroach, we may see ourselves more clearly. Even the most diminutive, even the gross, can become a source of wonder. In Lacy M. Johnson's essay "What Slime Knows," the author marvels at:

> a creature that begins life as a microscopic amoeba and ends it as a vibrant splotch that produces spores, and for all the time in between, it is a single cell that can grow as large as a bath mat, has no brain, no sense of sight or smell, but can solve mazes, learn patterns, keep time, and pass down the wisdom of generations.

The marvel of biodiversity on planet Earth begins with the very small. A recent calculation by a team of biologists and geologists, the *New York Times* reports, finds "there are more living cells on Earth—a million trillion trillion, or 10^{30} in math notation, a 1 followed by 30 zeros—than there are stars in the universe or grains of sand on our planet." Yet, the web of life is not a hierarchy. Everything is connected—that is ecology's clarion message. Every strand stitches together the fabric of life. To sing of the least among us is to celebrate this truth.

From the Hebrew Bible

In many traditions, wisdom is understood to be a possession of a god or gods. The gods confer on people only the quest for wisdom, knowing this must lead them back to the gods, for only the holy ones could possess wisdom. The quest itself had value, as it led people to the observational skills that have become science.

The book of Proverbs in the Hebrew Bible (also in the Christian Old Testament) offers instructions for living a moral and meaningful life. The purpose of the book is to teach people to seek wisdom as a way of living, a quest easily nudged aside amid daily distractions and folly. It holds that wisdom comes first from submission to God and cautions against taking the path of fools: "As a dog returns to his vomit, so a fool repeats his folly." The ant, on the other hand, offers a model of right living in harmony with nature.

GO TO THE ANT

Proverbs 6:6–8

Go to the ant, thou sluggard;
Consider her ways, and be wise:
Which having no guide, overseer,
    or ruler,
Provideth her meat in the summer, and
    gathereth her food in the harvest.

CHARACTERISTICS OF LIFE

"A fifth of animals without backbones could be at risk of
extinction, say scientists." —BBC *Nature News*

Ask me if I speak for the snail and I will tell you
   I speak for the snail.
                  I speak of underneathedness
and the welcome of mosses,
              of life that springs up,
little lives that pull back and wait for a moment.

I speak for the damselfly, water skeet, mollusk,
the caterpillar, the beetle, the spider, the ant.
                    I speak
from the time before spinelessness was frowned upon.

Ask me if I speak for the moon jelly. I will tell you
            one thing today and another tomorrow
   and I will be as consistent as anything alive
on this earth.

           I move as the currents move, with the breezes.
What part of your nature drives you? You, in your cubicle
ought to understand me. I filter and filter and filter all day.

Ask me if I speak for the nautilus and I will be silent
as the nautilus shell on a shelf. I can be beautiful
and useless if that's all you know to ask of me.

Ask me what I know of longing and I will speak of distances
between meadows of night-blooming flowers.
                    I will speak
        the impossible hope of the firefly.

                    You with the candle
burning and only one chair at your table must understand
such wordless desire.

        To say it is mindless is missing the point.

EXOTIC ANIMALS, BOOK FOR CHILDREN

Armadillo means
"little armored one."
Some of us become this to survive
in our own countries.
I would like to see an armadillo
crossing the road.
Our armor is invisible,
it polishes itself.
We might have preferred to be
a softer animal, wouldn't you?
With fur and delicate paws,
like an African Striped Grass Mouse,
also known as Zebra Mouse.

SCORPIONS

Scorpions have such big hearts,
my daughter tells me, pointing
to the diagram in her book.
Every winter, we gather them in glass jars.
My girl likes their utter
stillness, the way they rest harmless
until provoked. She is quiet, so fragile
she misses school some days
because she wakes crying and cannot stop.
Her brother teases her, his voice
sharp as the end of a stick.
Her anger is quick when she turns it on him
as the sudden whip when the scorpion
curls its tail over. The fat, venom tip
swaying just above the great heart.

ST. ROACH

For that I never knew you, I only learned to dread you,
for that I never touched you, they told me you are filth,
they showed me by every action to despise your kind;
for that I saw my people making war on you,
I could not tell you apart, one from another,
for that in childhood I lived in places clear of you,
for that all the people I knew met you by
crushing you, stamping you to death, they poured
    boiling water on you, they flushed you down,
for that I could not tell one from another
only that you were dark, fast on your feet, and slender.
  Not like me.
For that I did not know your poems
And that I do not know any of your sayings
And I cannot speak or read your language
And that I do not sing your songs
And that I do not teach our children
      to eat your food
      or know your poems
      or sing your songs
But that we say you are filthing our food
But that we know you not at all

Yesterday I looked at one of you for the first time.
You were lighter than the others in color, that was
  neither good nor bad.

I was really looking for the first time.
You seemed troubled and witty.

Today I touched one of you for the first time.
You were startled, you ran, you fled away
Fast as a dancer, light, strange and lovely to the touch.
I reach, I touch, I begin to know you.

WORKER

Clover whispers, each
lavender globe. Nine

days in the fields, then our wings

are shot. Day three
I came upon an orchid, hidden in
a stand of pine—newly opened,

mouth wide,

a lacy white corridor, heaven
after the gloom of the hive. Stumbling
inside, the scent

pulled me deeper, not caring
if she closed on me forever.

Francis Ponge
translated from the French by C. K. Williams

THE OYSTER

The oyster is about as large as a medium sized pebble, but rougher looking and less uniform in color, brilliantly whitish. An obstinately closed world, which, however, can be opened: grasp it in the hollow of a dishcloth, use a chipped, not too sharp knife, then give it a few tries. Prying fingers cut themselves on it, and break their nails: crude work. Blows mark its envelope with white circles, sorts of halos.

Inside, a whole world, both food and drink: under a firmament (strictly speaking) of mother of pearl, the heavens above sinking onto the heavens below form a mere puddle, a viscous, greenish sack fringed with blackish lace that ebbs and flows in your eyes and nostrils.

Sometimes, though rarely, a formula purls from its nacreous throat, which is immediately used as a personal adornment.

SLOTH SURPRISES

> "Like a rainbow before breakfast, a sloth is a surprise, an
> unexpected fellow breather of the air of our planet. No one
> could prophesy a sloth."   —William Beebe, *Jungle Days*

How would you feel hanging in cecropia trees
                until algae slicks your fur? Would you flinch
at being called a termite nest, a doormat draped

                around a branch, the mop-head butt of naturalist jokes?
("a masterpiece of immobility. . ." "an enthusiasm for life
                excelled by a healthy sunflower. . .

the second hand of a watch often covers
                more distance"). And what flips and flops
would your ego do if you were named in honour

                of a Deadly Sin? Its Spanish nickname
Perico Ligero (Nimble Peter), better praise than *Sloth*.
                Lethargy and listlessness are all

many think of it, lazily. Even a sloth website
                (yes, there are a few) kicks off with comedy:
the William Tell overture galloping

                from Packard Bell speakers. Pointing out
they sleep eighteen hours a day is like announcing
                dolphins leap, wolves howl, and gulls

tear garbage apart. What I want is what
                shakes up the known. Give me
the sport of snails, the mourning of sparrows,

            the rage of porcupines. I'm still waiting
to hear the worm that sings. Though no giraffe,
            the sloth could boast (if it chose to) the most

neck vertebrae of any mammal, the greatest range
            of temperatures. Caterpillars in its algae-matted coat
become moths that sip water from its nostrils and eyes.

            "Life disputes with death every inch of flesh . . .
I saw the heart of one beat for half an hour
            after it was taken out of the body."

And it swims, how it swims! When the Amazon
            rises higher, sloths cross a mile underwater
in no time, swinging their long forelimbs one

            after the other, blending dexterity and force.
Destined for other trees and camouflage,
            their hearts pick up speed, their great claws

cut water spangled with startled fish. All
            associations of sin wash from their thick fur.
Sloths swim with the might of eagles flying.

Manny Loley

BACK TO DENVER

for shicheii

Summer ends, and I am hurled
thousands of feet above the earth
in a metal tube. Outside, clouds.
Below, humans like ants
rush about in frantic motion.
My cheii liked to watch ants,
how they carried leaves and rocks
back to their homes. I never asked
why, but sat with him in the sun.
He was quiet and gentle, my cheii.
Back then, life was the mesa,
the light, and a spotless sky
we could get lost in, for days.
I couldn't believe it, he passed
and we buried him on the mesa.
After the burial, we swept
the earth, erasing our prints
from the sand. Nearby ants
carried white stones over
rippled sand dunes. We cried.
I think of my cheii, as I fly
over my homeland. In memory
the mesa looms, wrapped
in bright sunbeams, and I am
there. Warm sand between
my hands, rippled grasses
rippling into milkweed,

pine needles poke through
my jeans, and those red
flowers with white inside,
their petals sweet, on my tongue
like summer. In a metal tube,
I look out the window, pass
through clouds and think about
ants with white stones.

Rita Dove

THE SPRING CRICKET CONSIDERS THE QUESTION OF NEGRITUDE

I was playing my tunes all by myself;
I didn't know anybody else
who could play along.

Sure, the tunes were sad—
but sweet, too, and wouldn't come
until the day gave out. You know

that way the sky has of dangling
her last bright wisps? That's when
the ache would bloom inside

until I couldn't wait; I knelt down
to scrape myself clean
and didn't care who heard.

Then came the shouts and whistles,
the roundup into jars, a clamber of legs.
Now there were others: tumbled,

clouded. I didn't know their names.
We were a musical lantern;
children slept to our rasping sighs.

And if now and then one of us
shook free and sang as he climbed
to the brim, he would always

fall again. Which made them laugh
and clap their hands. At least then
we knew what pleased them,

and where the brink was.

Gerald Stern

I REMEMBER GALILEO

I remember Galileo describing the mind
as a piece of paper blown around by the wind,
and I loved the sight of it sticking to a tree
or jumping into the back seat of a car,
and for years I watched paper leap through my cities,
but yesterday I saw the mind was a squirrel caught crossing
Route 80 between the wheels of a giant truck,
dancing back and forth like a thin leaf,
or a frightened string, for only two seconds living
on the white concrete before he got away,
his life shortened by all that terror, his head
jerking, his yellow teeth ground down to dust.

It was the speed of the squirrel and his lowness to the ground,
his great purpose and the alertness of his dancing,
that showed me the difference between him and paper.

Paper will do in theory, when there is time
to sit back in a metal chair and study shadows;
but for this life I need a squirrel,
his clawed feet spread, his whole soul quivering,
the hot wind rushing through his hair,
the loud noise shaking him from head to tail.
    O philosophical mind, O mind of paper, I need a squirrel
finishing his wild dash across the highway,
rushing up his green ungoverned hillside.

PSEUDACRIS CRUCIFER

for Aaron

The father begins to make the sound a tree frog makes
When he comes with his son & daughter to a pail
Of tree frogs for sale in a Deep South flea market
Just before the last blood of dusk.
A tree frog is called a tree frog because it chirps
Like a bird in a tree, he tells his daughter
While her little brother, barely four years old,
Busies himself like a small blues piper
With a brand-new birthday harmonica.
A single tree frog can sound like a sleigh bell,
The father says. Several can sound like a choir
Of crickets. Once in high school, as I dissected
A frog, the frog opened its eyes to judge
Its deconstruction, its disassembly,
My scooping & poking at its soul.
And the little girl's eyes go wide as a tree frog's eyes.
Some call it the "spring peeper." In Latin
It's called *Pseudacris crucifer*. False locusts,
Toads with falsettos, their chimes issuing below
The low leaves & petals. The harmonica playing
Is so otherworldly, the boy blows with his eyes closed.
Some tree-frog species spend most every day
    underground.
They don't know what sunlight does at dusk.
They are nocturnal insectivores. No bigger than
A green thumb, they are the first frogs to call
In the spring. They may sound like crickets

Only because they eat so many crickets.
Tree frogs mostly sound like birds.
The tree frog overcomes its fear of birds by singing.
The harmonica playing is so bewitching,
The boy gathers a crowd in a flea market
In the Deep South. A bird may eat a frog.
A fox may eat the bird. A wolf may eat the fox.
And the wolf then may carry varieties of music
And cunning in its belly as it roams the countryside.
A wolf hungers because it cannot feel the good
In its body. The people clap & gather round
With fangs & smiles. The father lifts the son
To his shoulders so the boy's harmonics hover
Over varieties of affections, varieties of bodies
With their backs to a firmament burning & opening.
You can find damn near anything in a flea market:
Pets, weapons, flags, farm-fresh as well as farm-spoiled
Fruits & vegetables, varieties of old wardrobes,
A rusty old tin box with old postcards & old photos
Of lynchings dusted in the rust of the box.
You can feel it on the tips of your fingers,
This rust, which is almost as brown as the father
And the boy on his shoulders & the girl making
The sound a tree frog makes in a flea market
In the Deep South before the blood of dusk,
Just before the last blood of dusk. Just before the dusk.

MY PROTEINS

They have discovered, they say,
the protein of itch—
natriuretic polypeptide b—
and that it travels its own distinct pathway
inside my spine.
As do pain, pleasure, and heat.

A body it seems is a highway,
a cloverleaf crossing
well built, well traversed.
Some of me going north, some going south.

Ninety percent of my cells, they have discovered,
are not my own person,
they are other beings inside me.

As ninety-six percent of my life is not my life.

Yet I, they say, am they—
my bacteria and yeasts,
my father and mother,
grandparents, lovers,
my drivers talking on cell phones,
my subways and bridges,
my thieves, my police
who chase my self night and day.

My proteins, apparently also me,
fold the shirts.

I find in this crowded metropolis
a quiet corner,
where I build of not-me Lego blocks
a bench,
pigeons, a sandwich
of rye bread, mustard, and cheese.

It is me and is not,
the hunger
that makes the sandwich good.

It is not me then is,
the sandwich—
a mystery neither of us
can fold, unfold, or consume.

THE SACRED

erhaps the simplest definition of "the sacred" is that which we will not violate. "Is nothing sacred to you?" we say to the vilest among us. A hope of those who love animals and fear for their fate is that we love them enough to help them play out their full evolutionary potential, protected from the worst of human excess.

Thomas Berry's lifework was to bring together the spiritual and scientific views of the universe. A Catholic priest and scholar of world religions, he studied Earth's history and evolution, and he described himself as a "geologian." He wrote:

> The natural world is the larger sacred community to which we belong. To be alienated from this community is to become destitute in all that makes us human. To damage this community is to diminish our own existence.

Animals are sacred in many Indigenous traditions. The Yaqui of the desert Southwest and northern Mexico hold the deer as sacred. It inspires their Deer Songs and Deer Dance. For preconquest Mayan people, the jaguar could manifest as the Jaguar God of Terrestrial Fire, Jaguar God of the Underworld, Jaguar Goddess of Midwifery and War, and more. And for the Diné (Navajo people), the eagle has spiritual powers.

A feeling for the spiritual power of animals is captured in the Arabian proverb: "The wind of heaven is that which blows between a horse's ears." The cow is sacred in India, representing the divine and the maternal generosity of Nature. Killing a cow remained a capital offense for centuries, the animal becoming an inspiration for nonviolence. Poems from many traditions celebrate this sense that we are transformed in the presence of animals, that they lead us toward an experience of transcendence, of owning our desire for communion with the more-than-human world.

From Indigenous Traditions of the Pacific Northwest

The sacred finds a voice in prayer from many traditions, and prayer lies very close to poetry in its intensity, music, and emotion. Whether one prays to a raven, a salmon, or a saint, the intent is the same. Prayer bridges the gap between our inner lives and the great mystery of which we are a part, giving spiritual meaning to our longings.

When Richard Nelson wrote his book *Make Prayers to the Raven*, based on living and traveling with Koyukon people who followed a traditional way of life in Alaska, he was mindful of the limits of his understanding as an outsider and understood that anthropology could become an extractive practice. His "greatest wish," he wrote, "is that every page of this book reflect my admiration for them, should accurately record their teachings, and should have value and significance in their lives during these difficult times of change." His thinking marks a new era for ethnography based on mutual respect and conversation.

Nelson wrote that "the Koyukon people are helpless to change signs given them through natural spirits," but that, as a result of prayer, "these powerful spirits often show benevolence toward people." For example, when people see birds migrating south in the fall, "they may speak to them: 'I hope you will return again and that we will be here to see you.' It is a request that birds and people may survive the uncertainties of winter."

Nearly a century earlier, anthropologist Franz Boas was transcribing his interviews with the Kwakwaka'wakw people of the Pacific Northwest. Here, too, was a powerful testament to the spiritual connection between human and animal, and gratitude for the many ways their lives intertwined. Moved by these fragments, I adapted them into the poem "Prayer to the Sockeye Salmon," with the same hope and admiration as Nelson.

PRAYER TO THE SOCKEYE SALMON

from the Kwakwala

O, Swimmers, this is the dream
given by you, to be the way of my
late grandfathers when they first
caught you at your playground
in this river. Now you will be
in the same way, Swimmers.

I do not club you twice,
for I do not wish to club to death
your souls so that you may
go home to the place
where you come from, Supernatural Ones,
you, givers of heavy weight.

Thank you, Swimmers, you,
Supernatural Ones, that you have come
to try to save our lives,
mine and my husband's, that we
may not die of hunger, you
Long-Life-Maker, protect us,
that nothing evil may befall us, you,
Rich-Woman-Maker; and also
this, that we may meet again next year,
good, great Supernatural Ones.

EAGLE POEM

To pray you open your whole self
To sky, to earth, to sun, to moon
To one whole voice that is you.
And know there is more
That you can't see, can't hear,
Can't know except in moments
Steadily growing, and in languages
That aren't always sound but other
Circles of motion.
Like eagle that Sunday morning
Over Salt River. Circled in blue sky
In wind, swept our hearts clean
With sacred wings.
We see you, see ourselves and know
That we must take the utmost care
And kindness in all things.
Breathe in, knowing we are made of
All this, and breathe, knowing
We are truly blessed because we
Were born, and die soon within a
True circle of motion,
Like eagle rounding out the morning
Inside us.
We pray that it will be done
In beauty.
In beauty.

RETURNING

Bee Naanisdzá

Yisháálgo dólii bik'iniiyá
shitsijį' biinéé' hosoolts'ą́ą́'
  bee naanisdzá
diyingo biinéé' diists'ą́ą́'
  bee naanisdzá
dii bee shizaad hosoolts'įįl
  bee naanidszá
dii bee háhozhǫǫd
  hayíílką́ągo naanisdzá
  nííłtsą́zhool dah nida'ajoołgo naanisdzá

As I was walking, I came upon a bluebird
before me, bluebird's voice sounded
  I am returning
with holiness, bluebird's voice was heard
  I am returning
with this, my own voice sounds all around
  I am returning
with this, harmony fans out around me
  I am returning in a bright dawn
  I am returning in a light rain

Nickole Brown

A PRAYER TO TALK TO ANIMALS

Lord, I ain't asking to be the Beastmaster
gym-ripped in a jungle loincloth
or a Doctor Dolittle or even the expensive vet
down the street, that stethoscoped redhead,
her diamond ring big as a Cracker Jack toy.
All I want is for you to help me flip
off this lightbox and its scroll of dread, to rip
a tiny tear between this world and that, a slit
in the veil, Lord, one of those old-fashioned peeping
keyholes through which I can press my dumb
lips and speak. If you will, Lord, make me the teeth
hot in the mouth of a raccoon scraping
the junk I scraped from last night's plates,
make me the blue eye of that young crow cocked to
me—too selfish to even look up from the black
of my damn phone. Oh, forgive me, Lord,
how human I've become, busy clicking
what I like, busy pushing
my cuticles back and back to expose
all ten pale, useless moons. Would you let me
tell your creatures how sorry
I am, let them know exactly
what we've done? Am I not an animal
too? If so, Lord, make me one again.
Give me back my dirty claws and blood-warm
horns, braid back those long-
frayed endings of every nerve tingling
with all I thought I had to do today.

Fork my tongue, Lord. There is a sorrow on the air
I taste but cannot name. I want to open
my mouth and know the exact
flavor of what's to come, I want to open
my mouth and sound a language
that calls all language home.

COME INTO ANIMAL PRESENCE

Come into animal presence.
No man is so guileless as
the serpent. The lonely white
rabbit on the roof is a star
twitching its ears at the rain.
The llama intricately
folding its hind legs to be seated
not disdains but mildly
disregards human approval.
What joy when the insouciant
armadillo glances at us and doesn't
quicken his trotting
across the track into the palm brush.
What is this joy? That no animal
falters, but knows what it must do?
That the snake has no blemish,
that the rabbit inspects his strange surroundings
in white star-silence? The llama
rests in dignity, the armadillo
has some intention to pursue in the palm-forest.
Those who were sacred have remained so,
holiness does not dissolve, it is a presence
of bronze, only the sight that saw it
faltered and turned from it.
An old joy returns in holy presence.

ST KEVIN AND THE BLACKBIRD

And then there was St Kevin and the blackbird.
The saint is kneeling, arms stretched out, inside
His cell, but the cell is narrow, so

One turned-up palm is out the window, stiff
As a crossbeam, when a blackbird lands
and lays in it and settles down to nest.

Kevin feels the warm eggs, the small breast, the tucked
Neat head and claws and, finding himself linked
Into the network of eternal life,

Is moved to pity: now he must hold his hand
Like a branch out in the sun and rain for weeks
Until the young are hatched and fledged and flown.

*

And since the whole thing's imagined anyhow,
Imagine being Kevin. Which is he?
Self-forgetful or in agony all the time

From the neck on out down through his hurting forearms?
Are his fingers sleeping? Does he still feel his knees?
Or has the shut-eyed blank of underearth

Crept up through him? Is there distance in his head?
Alone and mirrored clear in love's deep river,
'To labour and not to seek reward,' he prays,

A prayer his body makes entirely
For he has forgotten self, forgotten bird
And on the riverbank forgotten the river's name.

BLESSING THE ANIMALS

Two by two, past
the portals of paradise,
camels & pythons parade.
As if on best behavior,
civil as robed billy goats
& Big Bird, they stroll
down aisles of polished stone
at the Feast of St. Francis.
An elephant daydreams, nudging
ancestral bones down a rocky path,
but won't venture near the boy
with the white mouse peeking
from his coat pocket. Beyond
monkeyshine, their bellows
& cries are like prayers
to unknown planets & zodiac
signs. The ferret & mongoose
on leashes, move as if they know
things with a sixth sense.
Priests twirl hoops of myrrh.
An Australian blue cattle dog
paces a heaven of memories—
a butterfly on a horse's ear
bright as a poppy outside
Urbino. As if crouched
between good & bad, St. John
the Divine grows in quintessence
& limestone, & a hoorah of Miltonic

light falls upon alley rats
awaiting nighttime. Brother
ass, brother sparrow hawk,
& brother dragon. Two
by two, washed & brushed down
by love & human pride,
these beasts of burden
know they're the first
scapegoats. After sacred
oils & holy water, we huddle
this side of their knowing
glances, & they pass through
our lives, still loyal to thorns.

GRIZZLY

She grazes in a meadow, sulphur blossoms spilling
from her jaw.

At this moment she seems so calm, she could be holy,
if what that means is something like being

wholly unaware of the good she gives,
how even her rooting tills the soil

and even her shitting ferries the seeds
and even her bathing is a joy to behold

as I am beholding her this morning
as she leans over a water hole, her shadow first

and then her reflection on the skin of the water,
then the splash as she enters, the pond opening,

rippling, and the scritch as she scrubs
her head with her paw, the great planet

of her head that she dunks and raises, shaking
the water in wide arcs, spraying

the lens of the hidden camera. And now
she climbs out, water rivering off her fur.

She is drying that huge head
in the long grasses.

And here she hunkers
over a bison carcass, slowly ripping free

the shoulder. Those precision instruments
that work with an ease that seems—yes—delicate.

Blood stains the river and stains
the snow bank and stains the rock.

Vessel carrying the chemicals of life—
hair and bone, flagella and bloom.

She carries them, lumbering forward
as she sinks her teeth and feeds.

Gerard Manley Hopkins

PIED BEAUTY

Glory be to God for dappled things—
  For skies of couple-colour as a brinded cow;
    For rose-moles all in stipple upon trout that swim;
Fresh-firecoal chestnut-falls; finches' wings;
  Landscape plotted and pieced—fold, fallow, and plough;
    And all trades, their gear and tackle and trim.

All things counter, original, spare, strange;
  Whatever is fickle, freckled (who knows how?)
    With swift, slow; sweet, sour; adazzle, dim;
He fathers-forth whose beauty is past change:
                    Praise him.

ANTHROPOCENE BLESSING: NIGHTJAR

Little goatsucker, bugeater,
you with moth bodies fluttering
their final moments in your bill.
You of the long, bark-mottled
wings. You of the broad-leafed
woods. In your crepuscular forays,
may each ghostling insect vanish
within your bristle-whiskered beak.
May the speckled eggs you lay
on the unnested leaf litter incubate
invisibly from mongeese, from
the jaws of feral cats. May you
distract our urban eyes from where
your cinnamon-downy chicks
fledge in the understory
by lifting your vibrating form
in conspicuous flight. Little
nighthawk, may your whip-noted
voice infiltrate the limestone
world. Tucuchillo, may your
metallic song be a knife ascending
in the darkness, protecting your
thorny thickets from the forest
mulcher's spinning slice.

Robinson Jeffers

VULTURE

I had walked since dawn and lay down to rest on a bare hillside
Above the ocean. I saw through half-shut eyelids a vulture wheeling high up in heaven,
And presently it passed again, but lower and nearer, its orbit narrowing,
     I understood then
That I was under inspection. I lay death still and heard the flight-feathers
Whistle above me and make their circle and come nearer.
I could see the naked red head between the great wings
Bear downward staring. I said, "My dear bird, we are wasting time here.
These old bones will still work; they are not for you."
But how beautiful he looked, gliding down
On those great sails; how beautiful he looked, veering
away in the sea-light over the precipice. I tell you solemnly
That I was sorry to have disappointed him. To be eaten
by that beak and become part of him, to share those wings and those eyes—
What a sublime end of one's body, what an enskyment;
What a life after death.

LIKE JESUS TO THE CROWS

that gathered there along his arms,
upon the invitation of a slender limb.
And not oblivious to human violence
perhaps needed rest or needed to offer
the succor of presence, despite the
stiff collar of their feathers, despite
each one being no less the children
of a father who claimed an upper realm.

It is not true they pecked his eyes. Nor
did they consider his wounds
their own. They were neither irreverent
nor quiet. They spoke in the tongues
they knew. They cawed full voiced
and would have released him from his
bindings had their beaks held the power
and had there been time in that place.

Like them, I have sought to comfort and
so be comforted. Like them
I have seen the failure of miracles when
they were most needed. Like Him, I
have called upon those so unlike myself
when my father failed to answer.

Derek Sheffield

CONTEXTUAL EDUCATION

Wenatchee, Washington

"He wouldn't make us like *monkeys!*"
says a student in the front row.
"'Cause he made us in *his* image."
She laughs and turns to check
for smiles and nods. The professor
stands by the whiteboard
where he has written the word
adaptation. He is thinking of all
the lessons, like similes,
that have appeared in black ink
across this space,
and that have, like species,
gone. He cannot help
but see her in the church van
on the field trip, pretending
she doesn't know she's the pretty one
who doesn't know exactly
what's happening inside the boy
beside her when she tosses
her pink-streaked hair and blows
a word across his ear. In the room's silence,
she shows them what she means
by turning her hands into big ears
and wagging her head side to side.

They wonder if they are some sort
of experiment as their professor
turns off the lights and clicks
a chimp's face onto the screen.
No one says a thing
at the god looking back
from those brown, sad eyes.

Stanley Kunitz

THE SNAKES OF SEPTEMBER

All summer I heard them
rustling in the shrubbery,
outracing me from tier
to tier in my garden,
a whisper among the viburnums,
a signal flashed from the hedgerow,
a shadow pulsing
in the barberry thicket.
Now that the nights are chill
and the annuals spent,
I should have thought them gone,
in a torpor of blood
slipped to the nether world
before the sickle frost.
Not so. In the deceptive balm
of noon, as if defiant of the curse
that spoiled another garden,
these two appear on show
through a narrow slit
in the dense green brocade
of a north-country spruce,
dangled head-down, entwined
in a brazen love-knot.
I put out my hand and stroke
the fine, dry grit of their skins.

After all,
we are partners in this land,
co-signers of a covenant.
At my touch the wild
braid of creation
trembles.

THE FUTURE OF ANIMALS

"Biodiversity," wrote the great biologist E. O. Wilson, "is the key to the maintenance of the world as we know it. Life in a local site struck down by a passing storm springs back quickly because enough diversity still exists." After an asteroid six miles wide crashed into Earth 66 million years ago, the climate changes were so extreme that dinosaurs became extinct. Wilson describes the force of impact as "greater than the detonation of all the nuclear weapons in the world. It rang the earth, like a bell, ignited wildfires, washed the shore with giant tsunamis, and kicked up an immense dust cloud that enshrouded the planet." That was the fifth time in the planet's history that so much life was lost. Only a few small mammals existed at the time, but with the dinosaurs gone, they had an opportunity to thrive. It took time. Wilson estimates it takes five million years for biodiversity to recover after a major extinction event.

Lucky for us that the age of mammals did so well. One mammal in particular, one that's been around for only about the past two hundred thousand years, has taken off like wildfire. So much so that scientists from around the world have named our epoch the Anthropocene—the age of humans.

With all of our marvelous human talents and ideals, we have had a staggering impact on other creatures. We stand on the edge of the sixth mass extinction, with animals falling into extinction one thousand times faster than they would without human impacts. Since 1970, the population of wild animals has decreased by two-thirds, while the human population has doubled. This is a profoundly unsettling reality to come to terms with, an incomprehensible loss, because we love animals. The biodiverse Earth is where the human spirit was nurtured. We call her Mother Earth. The diminishment of the creaturely world is a diminishment of our family.

The work of poets is to tell us how it feels to be alive at this time in history as opposed to any other. Animals enter our poems as thought experiments about what the future might hold. Extinction looms, but so, too, does that force of life that drives creatures to adapt and survive.

From Ancient Greek Philosophy

The pre-Socratic philosopher Empedocles was born into a wealthy family in Greek Sicily. Poet and translator Dan Beachy-Quick, in his book *The Thinking Root,* writes of Empedocles's generous nature: "to poor brides he gave a dowry." His philosophy centered on the tension of two opposing forces: Love and Strife. His biography is filled with legends and unknowns: He may have lived to be sixty—or past one hundred.

Empedocles described a continuity between humans and animals, and he believed that to kill and eat an animal was cannibalism. He became a vegetarian and was opposed to animal sacrifice. This sense of the interconnectedness inherent in nature, written into verses in the fifth century BCE, lays a seedbed for contemporary ecological thought.

While the extinction of our animal kin is dispiriting for our time, this brief excerpt from an ancient philosopher's thinking reminds us in poetic terms that in nature all is change. Nature is in a constant process of reinvention. She meets each disturbance with a renewal of life's potential: new forms, new species, new communities of interrelationship.

FROM EMPEDOCLES

from the ancient Greek

I'll tell you another thing: in nature there is never
all dying, the world doesn't end in one final wretched death—
but only mixing, separating, and gathering up again
is what is. What humans name nature is this motion.

David Baker

EXTINCTION

When you are gone they will read your footprints,
if they still read, as they might a poem about love—
wandering in circles, here and there obscured,
washed out in places by weather, sudden landslide.
Keep walking, pilgrim. This is your great tale.

Anne Haven McDonnell

THE SWIMMERS

After all the wolves on the island were killed by cyanide, traps, and bullets,
    decades later, wolves
from the mainland swam for miles to repopulate the island.
By dream, by twitch, by lope, by gazing from the shore, by howls that gather,
    by circle and whine,
by hint, rumor and surge, by yearn, nip, and bark, by stretch, itch, and shake,
by splash, dunk, and swim by starlight, by bull kelp and driftwood, by calm
and gelatinous sea, by stink of whale, by salt of far, by winter fur, by paws
as paddles, by chuff and nostril huff, by steam of breath above the sea,
by belly of salmon, by hunger for deer, by memory in blood,
by roam for love, by milk and teat, by marrow and fat,
by muscle, skull and golden eyes, by magnetic pull,
by currents and tides, by miles, by sinking
cold, with no one watching
by sea by sea by sea.

Brenda Hillman

SPECIES PREPARE TO EXIST AFTER MONEY

Turns out bacteria communicate in color.
  They warn each other in teal
  or celadon & humans assign
meaning to this, saying they are distressed
      or full of longing. The wood rat
    makes a nest of H's; it hoards
the seven tiny silences. Crows in the pine
can count specific faces like writers
    who feel their art has been ignored.
        My father spent his life thinking
      about money though he knew
      it causes most of this stupid violence,

& he thought of me as a sensible person;
    you have the chemical for sensible, he said.
There was no tragedy between us,
        unlike how poor Joyce wrote
      that his daughter turned away
from *that battered cabman's face, the world.*
  i didn't turn away because i don't know
where it is, it is all over, & when it seems
    pure nothingness has come to pass,
i know another animal prepares itself
      nationless, not sensible;
        thinking of it helps a little bit—

from LOOK AT THIS BLUE

we need balance. Need keep from
what may kill us all   what may
end us.   Distinguish an atom, a
gathered molecule, something we must
in each and every touch in this life in
every single moment of solitude and in
silence in the coming and going of River and her
embodiment of so many other beings she
nurtures to replenish us with the life givers the
fish she bears and birds who seek her
for snails and protection as we seek River for
healing to rekindle us in our own winterings.
Now is the time to return to what we do with
our partnerships in life, the cranes impressing
us for generation upon generation giving us
dances and life and reason and approach to
enjoy the reason we were gifted these particular atoms.

Rebecca Morgan Frank

NOT EVERYBODY'S BESTIARY (YET)

Then came the soft animals, the snake
and octopus, slinking along. You've seen
the octopus as escape artist, sneaking out
of cracks and holes, hiding in a tea pot,
plotting the big adventure. Now she moves
through chemical reaction, the first soft
robot, taking to the sea. Remember
that the real thing once disassembled
her own aquarium, waiting, bemused,
in the remaining puddle, for her custodian
to come. They say it was simply curiosity.
Now imagine her robot double dismantling
at will. That which we have tried to contain,
swimming off into the deep, re-emerging

like the snake that slithers into your garden;
its trapezoidal kirigami cuts in plastic skin
keep it crawling through bursts of air.
An innocuous slinky in colorful garb,
this robot can sidewind anywhere.
Now ask why everything now harbors
a weapon in your mind—do you dread
the snake under your own bed?
Is it the real tooth and venom you fear,
or this programmed body double here?

We're told of a fall, a fault built on flesh—
the flesh of a fruit, the flesh of a woman—
now this manmade flesh, a reptilian test
of applied knowledge. Industrial sin

co-starring the latest sensation: a running
cockroach robot, sliding through cracks
to get to you, away from you, through
your walls. Extinction now eradicated,
bought: replacements on order. Enter
"Robotanica"—the world of the wild robot—
woodpecker, dragonfly, kangaroo, child—
unborn, they can all do the job. Two by two,
battery-powered to keep the world moving,
replacing their organic prototypes. Centipedes,
spiders, ants, termites, and robobees, these
are just the beginning of the evolving nation,
as if someone has decided to revise, start over.
This time using human labor, invention.

PLAYING WITH BEES

So the world turned
its one good eye

to watch the bees
take most of metaphor
with them.

Swarms—
in all their airborne
pointillism—
shifted on the breeze

for the last time. Of course,
the absence of bees
left behind significant holes
in ecology. Less

obvious
were the indelible holes
in poems, which would come
later:

Our vast psychic habitat
shrunk. Nothing was

like nectar

for the gods

Nobody was warned by
a deep black dahlia, and nobody

grew like a weed.

Nobody felt spry as
　　　　　　　a daisy, or blue
　　　　　　　and princely
as a hyacinth; was lucid as
　　　　　　　a moon flower.　　Nobody came home

　　　　　　　and yelled *honey!* up the stairs,

And nothing in particular
by any other name would smell as sweet as—

Consider:
the verbal dearth
that is always a main ripple of extinction.

The lexicon of wilds goes on nixing its descriptions.
Slimming its index of references
for what is

super as a rhubarb, and juicy
as a peach,
or sunken as a
comb and ancient as an alder tree, or
conifer, or beech, what is royal
as jelly, dark as a wintering

hive, toxic as the jessamine vine
who weeps the way a willow does,
silently as wax
burned in the land of milk and—

all the strong words in poems,
they were once

smeared on the mandible of a bee.

DEAR FISHER CAT (*MARTES PENNANTI*)

Never seen you in the flesh. I've seen
a cousin, *Martes martes*, stuffed, in a shop window
in Bavaria, where they chew wiring in cars,
and *Martes zibellina* turned
into a coat, thicker than mink, the price of a house.
I tried it on, with awe.
I watched *Martes fiona* on YouTube,
the woman holding the camera cooing
while the small, shy animal
nosed around her terrace in the English countryside.
Your name in Croatian, Kuna, is currency.
Seven million years old, much older than *Homo*,
and certainly *sapiens*. Trapped to the brink
of extinction, you came back.
You are to the others as the javelina is to the wild boar,
a new world clade. Neither fisher nor cat.
Some people love bears or whales
or whooping cranes; I love you:
your sweet round ears and button nose,
your fur heavy as the robe of a queen,
your claws unsheathed in paws
the size of a child's hand. You could be a toy, a cartoon,
a pet, if it weren't for your carnivorous drive,
your solitary soul. Your jaws can kill a porcupine,
attacking snout first from below, eating it inside
out. You cross the narrowest gap
in the forest opening. You sleep in the crook
of a beech in old-growth canopy. I'll see you someday,

close range. I'll be the rabbit
curled in the corner of the parsley garden
and you—you'll be there, unnoticed
until too late, to swallow all the sounds my gullet makes.

Homero Aridjis
translated from the Spanish by George McWhirter

THE CREATION OF THE WORLD BY THE ANIMALS

(according to the Popol Vuh)

Across an empty darkness,
across unmoving sky,
flashed scarlet macaw—
so day broke; and yellow orioles
with turquoise eyes
began dancing a solo of light

and within a mighty ceiba tree,
the "mother of birds," appeared
a skinny spider monkey
his privates dangling—and howler monkey,
scriving prophecies on the mirror of dawn,
and a lunar owl, perched on death's arm.

Caiman lurked on a river bank,
his back marked with celestial stripes,
and sharp-fanged jaguar
pursued the fleeing deer; and eagle,
aloft on clear wings, spied the horizon—
and all was a feathered dream: yellow and green.

Then figured from water, clay, and wood,
came woman and man:
offspring of the sun,
children of forest and mountain,
with their eyes they could behold themselves,
their voices named the animals.

Heart of the Sky, Heart of the Sea
Heart of the Earth beat as one,
and all the winged creatures, creatures
of the waters and the land
could be, breathe, love, and cast shade.
And life is re-created every day.

CAN YOU

hear yourself
breathe. Can you help
me. Can you
hear the fly. Can you

hear the tree. No
I don't mean wind,
I mean the breathing of
the tree through

bark. Can u, say the grasses
please hear
us. Can we hear u hear
the tips of water on

us, lithe &
so heavy with light & bending
lens-tips. Can u
hear this e-

vaporation. Can u
keep
blessing, keep not
thinking, remind

yourself of

your own

breathing, & what
is growing—leaves root sap, sun
forcing the flower. . . .
Moving this way

you'll see you can hear
soil breathe,
& in it, working to get thru it,
the worm,

& each turning of it
by the worm, hear, &
the breathing in it
of the worm, hear. Moving this way

you'll hear the earth go on
without you—
when u are
no longer

here, when u are

not breathing. The fish the
water sand the
needle in the pine. The here. Hear it
breathing

as it turns,
and as now in it turns
the effort
of this worm.

IF PAST BECOMES FUTURE

Under their fast sky, some still
Will flit, clever bodies and light

Invisible among the leaves—or,

If their beloved trees have not
Returned, some will burrow

Or bower; some winkle from

The roots of grasses bugs that also
Escaped, and seeds, or learn to sip new

Nectars dreamed up by whatever flowers

Become. Those blooms, insects, whatever
Birds call themselves wear colors

We can't imagine, not that we see

The world well now, having never before
Needed accurate vision. Consider who

We mourn in advance. We grew up

Alongside, on them cultivated
Love for heart-catch and grandeur,

Named them. When we go,

Who do the small and quick fan
Their wings for, flashing eyes? Who do

They preen for now—

170

CONTRIBUTORS

INDRAN AMIRTHANAYAGAM is a poet, editor, publisher, translator, YouTube host, and diplomat. The author of 24 poetry books, he writes in English, Spanish, French, Portuguese, and Haitian Creole. He edits *Beltway Poetry Quarterly*; writes a weekly poem for *Haiti en Marche* and *El Acento*; and has received fellowships from the Foundation for the Contemporary Arts, the New York Foundation for the Arts, the US-Mexico Fund for Culture, and the MacDowell Colony. His most recent books in English are *The Runner's Almanac* (Spuyten Duyvil, 2024) and *Seer* (Hanging Loose Press, 2024).

HOMERO ARIDJIS, one of Latin America's foremost literary figures, has written 51 books of poetry and prose, including the 2023 collection *Self-Portrait in the Zone of Silence*, translated from the Spanish by **GEORGE McWHIRTER**, winner of the Griffin Poetry Prize. Former ambassador to Switzerland, the Netherlands, and UNESCO, Aridjis is also president emeritus of PEN International and founder and president of the Group of 100, an environmental association of artists and scientists.

DAVID BAKER is the author of 12 books of poetry, most recently *Whale Fall* and *Swift: New & Selected Poems*. He has also written six prose books about poetry. His honors include fellowships from the Guggenheim Foundation and the National Endowment for the Arts. He lives and teaches in Granville, Ohio.

BRIAN BARTLETT has published 16 collections and chapbooks of poetry, 3 prose books of nature writing, and a gathering of prose on poetry. He has also edited several selections by Canadian poets, as well as Alden Nowlan's *Collected Poems*. His most recent books are *Daystart Songflight: A Morning Journal* and *The Astonishing Room*. He has lived in Kjipuktuk/Halifax since 1990.

ELLEN BASS'S most recent poetry collection is *Indigo*. Among her awards are fellowships from the Guggenheim Foundation and the National Endowment for the Arts, as well as the Lambda Literary Award and four Pushcart Prizes. She coedited the first major anthology of women's poetry, *No More Masks!*, and coauthored the groundbreaking *The Courage to Heal*. A chancellor emerita of the Academy of American Poets, Bass founded poetry workshops at Salinas Valley State Prison and the Santa Cruz jails, and she teaches in Pacific University's MFA program.

FRANCESCA BELL is the author of *Bright Stain*, a finalist for the Washington State Book Award and the Julie Suk Award, and *What Small Sound*. She translated *Whoever Drowned Here* by German poet Max Sessner. She is the poet laureate of Marin County, California.

WENDELL BERRY is the author of more than 30 books of poetry, fiction, and essays. An elder statesman of American environmental writing, he has been honored with fellowships from the Guggenheim and Rockefeller Foundations and the National Endowment for the Arts, as well as a Lannan Literary Award. He lives on a farm in Port Royal, Kentucky.

KIMBERLY BLAESER, past Wisconsin Poet Laureate and founding director of Indigenous Nations Poets, is the author of six poetry collections—most recently *Ancient Light* and the bilingual *Résister en dansant/Ikwe-niimi: Dancing Resistance*. An enrolled member of the White Earth Nation, she is an Anishinaabe activist and environmentalist. Blaeser serves as the 2024 Mackey Chair in Creative Writing at Beloit College and is an MFA faculty member at the Institute of American Indian Arts and a professor emerita at the University of Wisconsin-Milwaukee.

ELIZABETH BRADFIELD'S most recent books are *Toward Antarctica*, *Once Removed*, and *Cascadia Field Guide: Art, Ecology, Poetry*. Her honors include the Audre Lorde Award for Lesbian Poetry and a Stegner Fellowship. She works as a naturalist and field assistant, teaches creative writing at Brandeis University, and is editor in chief of Broadsided Press. Learn more at ebradfield.com.

TINA MOZELLE BRAZIEL is the author of *Known by Salt* (Anhinga Press), winner of the Philip Levine Prize for Poetry. She has been awarded an artist residency at Hot Springs National Park, a fellowship from the Alabama State Council on the Arts, and the inaugural Eco-Poetry Fellowship from the Magic City Poetry Festival. She and her husband, writer James Braziel, wrote *Glass Cabin* (Pulley Press), about how they live in a glass cabin that they are building by hand.

NICKOLE BROWN is the author of *Sister*, first published in 2007 and reissued in 2018. Her second book, *Fanny Says* (BOA Editions), won the Weatherford Award for Appalachian Poetry in 2015. She teaches at the Sewanee School of Letters MFA Program and lives in Asheville, North Carolina, where she volunteers at several animal sanctuaries. Since 2016, she's been writing about these animals. *To Those Who Were Our First Gods*, a chapbook of these first nine poems, won the 2018 Rattle Prize, and her essay in poems, *The Donkey Elegies*, was published by Sibling Rivalry Press in 2020. She's the president of the Hellbender Gathering of Poets, an annual environmental literary festival set to launch in Black Mountain, North Carolina, in October 2025.

YOSA BUSON (1716–1784) was a Japanese poet and painter of the Edo period. Along with Matsuo Basho and Kobayashi Issa, he is considered among the greatest poets of the haiku and haibun forms. During his lifetime he was more widely respected as a painter in the haiga style. Translator **ROBERT HASS** is a renowned poet who served as US Poet Laureate from 1995 to 1997. His work has won the

National Book Award, the Pulitzer Prize, and the Wallace Stevens Award from the Academy of American Poets.

JOHN CLARE (1793–1864) was a major nineteenth-century English poet whom Carolyn Kizer called "the most neglected great poet in our language." His biographer Jonathan Bate called Clare "the greatest labouring-class poet that England has ever produced. No one has ever written more powerfully of nature, of a rural childhood, and of the alienated and unstable self." Clare was treated in literary circles with condescension as a peasant, though he read Shakespeare and wrote sonnets as well as poems of witness to rural life and the displacement of the poor.

LUCILLE CLIFTON (1936–2010) was a prolific and widely esteemed poet, many of whose works focus on her experience as a Black woman in America. She was discovered as a poet by Langston Hughes. Among her honors were the National Book Award and serving as a chancellor for the Academy of American Poets. She was Distinguished Professor of Humanities at St. Mary's College in Maryland.

KATHARINE COLES has written 10 poetry collections, including her latest, *Time and Chance* (Turtle Point Press, April 2025). Her prose books include *The Stranger I Become: On Walking, Looking, and Writing* (essays), *Look Both Ways* (memoir), and two novels. She served as poet laureate of Utah and as poet in residence at the Natural History Museum of Utah and the Salt Lake City Public Library for the Poets House Field Work program. She has received awards from the National Endowment for the Arts, the National Endowment for the Humanities, the National Science Foundation's Antarctic Artists and Writers Program, and the Guggenheim Foundation. She is a distinguished professor at the University of Utah.

MICHAEL COLLIER'S most recent book is *The Missing Mountain: New and Selected Poems* (2021). A recipient of fellowships from the National Endowment for the Arts and the Rockefeller and Guggenheim Foundations, as well as an award in literature from the American Academy of Arts and Letters, he is a professor emeritus of English at the University of Maryland and a director emeritus of the Middlebury College Bread Loaf Writers' Conferences.

BRITTNEY CORRIGAN is the author of the poetry collections *Daughters*, *Breaking*, *Navigation*, *40 Weeks*, and most recently *Solastalgia*, a collection of poems about climate change, extinction, and the Anthropocene Age (JackLeg Press, 2023). She was raised in Colorado and has lived in Portland, Oregon, for the past three decades, where she is an alumna and employee of Reed College. Corrigan is currently at work on her first short story collection. For more information, visit brittneycorrigan.com.

KAMELLA CRUZ is from Ohkay Owingeh Pueblo, *Village of the Strong People*. She is the matriarch and mother of four children. She received her BFA in creative writing from the Institute of American Indian Arts after studying fiction, screenwriting, journalism, poetry, and nonfiction. Cruz is currently a graduate student at IAIA, where she is obtaining her MFA in poetry. She holds three national creative writing awards from *Tribal College Journal* (2022): best fiction, best poetry, and best nonfiction. She was also a nominee for the 2022 Pushcart Prize in poetry. Cruz writes for the mothers and grandmothers before her.

TODD DAVIS is the author of eight books of poetry, most recently *Ditch Memory: New & Selected Poems* and *Coffin Honey*. He has won the Midwest Book Award, the Foreword INDIES Book of the Year Award, and the Gwendolyn Brooks Poetry Award. He is an emeritus fellow of the Black Earth Institute and teaches environmental studies at Pennsylvania State University's Altoona College.

ALISON HAWTHORNE DEMING'S sixth poetry collection is *Blue Flax and Yellow Mustard Flower* (Red Hen Press, 2025). Her first book, *Science and Other Poems*, won the Walt Whitman Award from the Academy of American Poets. She is also author of five nonfiction books, including *A Woven World: On Fashion, Fishermen, and the Sardine Dress* and *Zoologies: On Animals and the Human Spirit*. With Lauret E. Savoy, she coedited the anthology *The Colors of Nature: Culture, Identity, and the Natural World*. Deming served as poet in residence at the Jacksonville Zoo and Gardens in Florida for the Poets House Language of Conservation project, and also at the Milwaukee Public Museum and the Milwaukee Public Library for the Poets House Field Work program. Her awards include a Guggenheim Fellowship, Wallace Stegner Fellowship at Stanford University, and two National Endowment for the Arts fellowships. Deming is Regents Professor Emerita at the University of Arizona.

TOI DERRICOTTE, poet, educator, and memoirist, has published six poetry collections, most recently *I: New & Selected Poems* in 2019. Her work has earned many honors, including the 2020 Frost Medal for Distinguished Lifetime Achievement in Poetry, the 2021 Wallace Stevens Award from the Academy of American Poets, and the 2023 Pegasus Award for Service in Poetry. With Cornelius Eady, she cofounded Cave Canem.

JOSE HERNANDEZ DIAZ is a 2017 National Endowment for the Arts poetry fellow. He is the author of *The Fire Eater* (Texas Review Press, 2020); *Bad Mexican, Bad American* (Acre Books, 2024); *The Parachutist* (Sundress Publications, 2025); and *Portrait of the Artist as a Brown Man* (Red Hen Press, 2025). He teaches generative workshops for Hugo House, Lighthouse Writers Workshops, the Writer's Center, and elsewhere.

EMILY DICKINSON (1830–1886), considered one of the most important American poets, published only 10 of her estimated 1,800 poems during her lifetime. She was born to a prominent family in Amherst, Massachusetts, educated at Amherst Academy and Mount Holyoke Female Seminary, and spent her life in her family's home.

MARK DOTY is the author of nine books of poetry, including *Deep Lane* (2015); *Fire to Fire: New and Selected Poems*, which won the 2008 National Book Award; and *My Alexandria*, winner of the *Los Angeles Times* Book Prize, the National Book Critics Circle Award, and the T. S. Eliot Prize. He is also the author of four memoirs: the *New York Times* bestseller *Dog Years*, *What Is the Grass*, *Firebird*, and *Heaven's Coast*, as well as a book about craft and criticism, *The Art of Description: World into Word*. Doty has received two National Endowment for the Arts fellowships, Guggenheim and Rockefeller Foundation fellowships, a Lila Wallace-Readers Digest Award, and the Witter Bynner Prize.

RITA DOVE served as US Poet Laureate from 1993 to 1995. She received the National Humanities Medal from President Bill Clinton and the National Medal of Arts from President Barack Obama—the only poet ever to receive both. Besides 29 honorary degrees from institutions including Harvard and Yale Universities, her honors include the 2019 Wallace Stevens Award, the American Academy of Arts and Letters 2021 Gold Medal for Poetry, a 2022 Ruth Lilly Poetry Prize, the Bobbitt Prize for lifetime achievement from the Library of Congress, and the 2023 Medal for Distinguished Contribution to American Letters from the National Book Foundation. Her numerous books include *Thomas and Beulah* (winner of the 1987 Pulitzer Prize), *On the Bus with Rosa Parks*, *Sonata Mulattica*, *Collected Poems 1974–2004*, and *Playlist for the Apocalypse*. Her play *The Darker Face of the Earth* was staged at the Kennedy Center in Washington, D.C., and the National Theatre in London, and her song cycles with composers John Williams, Tania Leon, Richard Danielpour, and others were performed at Tanglewood, Lincoln Center in New York, and the Kennedy Center. Dove teaches creative writing at the University of Virginia.

CAMILLE DUNGY'S poetry and prose considers history, landscape, culture, family, and desire. Her latest book is *Soil: The Story of a Black Mother's Garden*. Dungy is the author of four collections of poetry, most recently *Trophic Cascade*, winner of the Colorado Book Award. She also edited the groundbreaking anthology *Black Nature: Four Centuries of African American Nature Poetry*.

EMPEDOCLES (~492–432 BCE) was a pre-Socratic philosopher who recorded his ideas in verse. A follower of Pythagoras, a vegetarian, and a healer who claimed he could revive the dead and control wind and rain, he came up with the concept of the four elements of matter: earth, fire, water, air. Translator **DAN BEACHY-QUICK** is a poet and essayist who sought the poetry in early Greek philosophy and gathered it in his book *The Thinking Root*.

ENHEDUANA (~2300 BCE) is the first poet whose name we know, as translator **SOPHUS HELLE** describes her. A high priestess and royal princess living in Ur (now southern Iraq), her poems were originally inscribed on clay tablets. They speak of exile, social upheaval, the power of story, gender roles, the devastation of war, and the frightening forces of nature. Helle is a writer, translator, and cultural historian.

RK FAUTH is the author of *A Dream in Which I Am Playing with Bees*, winner of the Walt MacDonald First Book Prize in Poetry (Texas Tech University Press, 2024). Her writing has appeared or is forthcoming in *Poetry*, the Academy of American Poets Poem-a-Day, *AGNI*, and elsewhere. Fauth's work is anthologized in Jacar Press's *Dream of the River*, an LGBTQ poetry collection, and *The West Trade Review*'s *Ecobloomspaces*. She has received fellowships and writing awards from the Academy of American Poets, the US Fulbright Program, the Oak Spring Garden Foundation, the North Carolina Poetry Society, and the Lannan Center for Poetics and Social Practice. She lives in Asheville, North Carolina.

LAWRENCE FERLINGHETTI (1919–2021) founded, with Peter D. Martin, the legendary San Francisco bookstore City Lights. His 1958 poetry collection, *A Coney Island of the Mind*, sold over one million copies in the United States and abroad. Ferlinghetti's numerous awards included the National Book Critics Circle's Ivan Sandrof Lifetime Achievement Award, the Poetry Society of America's Frost Medal, and the National Book Foundation's Literarian Award. He was named commandeur of the French Order of Arts and Letters, among other honors.

EDWARD FIELD is the author of 10 books of poetry, 2 of nonfiction, and 3 of fiction with his partner, Neil Derrick, among other works. Field has been honored with the Lamont Poetry Prize, the Prix de Rome, a Guggenheim Fellowship, and a Lambda Literary Award.

NICK FLYNN is the author of six collections of poetry, all published by Graywolf, including *I Will Destroy You* (2019) and *Low* (2023). His best-selling memoir *Another Bullshit Night in Suck City* (Norton, 2004), was made into a film starring Robert DeNiro (Focus Features, 2012) and has been translated into 15 languages. Learn more at nickflynn.org.

VIEVEE FRANCIS is the author of *Blue-Tail Fly* (Wayne State University Press, 2006), *Horse in the Dark* (Northwestern University Press, 2012), and *Forest Primeval* (Northwestern University Press, 2016). She is also the winner of the Kingsley Tufts Poetry Award and the Hurston/Wright Legacy Award for Poetry. She is an associate professor at Dartmouth College and an associate editor for *Callaloo*.

REBECCA MORGAN FRANK is the author of *The Spokes of Venus*, *Sometimes We're All Living in a Foreign Country*, and *Oh You Robot Saints!*, all from Carnegie Mellon University Press, and *Little Murders Everywhere* (Salmon Poetry).

JORIE GRAHAM is the author of 15 poetry collections, most recently *To 2040*. Her poetry has been widely translated and has received many awards, including the Pulitzer Prize, the Forward Prize (UK), the Los Angeles Times Book Award, the International Nonino Prize, and the Rebekah Johnson Bobbitt National Prize for Poetry from the Library of Congress. She teaches at Harvard University.

THOM GUNN (1929–2004), English poet and essayist, relocated to San Francisco to study with Ivor Winters. His book *The Man with Night Sweats* spoke powerfully to the losses of the early AIDS crisis. The book won the 1994 Lenore Marshall Poetry Prize. Among other honors, he received Guggenheim and MacArthur Fellowships.

JOY HARJO, the 23rd US Poet Laureate and member of the Muscogee Nation, is the author of 10 books of poetry, as well as plays, children's books, and two memoirs. She was recently honored with the Frost Medal from the Poetry Society of America, Yale's 2023 Bollingen Prize for American Poetry, and the National Book Critics Circle Ivan Sandrof Lifetime Achievement Award. As a musician, Harjo has produced seven award-winning music albums. She is the inaugural artist in residence for Tulsa's Bob Dylan Center and lives on the Muscogee Nation Reservation in Oklahoma.

TERRANCE HAYES is the author of *American Sonnets for My Past and Future Assassin* (winner of the 2019 Hurston/Wright Legacy Award), *Lighthead* (winner of the 2010 National Book Award), *So to Speak*, and *Watch Your Language: Visual & Literary Reflections on a Century of American Poetry*, in addition to other works of poetry and prose. His honors include fellowships from the Guggenheim and MacArthur Foundations. He teaches at New York University.

SEAMUS HEANEY (1939–2013) was an Irish poet, playwright, and translator. Considered one of the major poets of the twentieth century, he received the 1995 Nobel Prize in Literature.

ALLISON ADELLE HEDGE COKE'S recent honors include the Thomas Wolfe Prize, a Legacy Artist fellowship from the California Arts Council, a Fulbright Scholarship, the George Garrett Award, the First Jade Nurtured SiHui Female International Poetry Award, Mellon Dean's Professorship at the University of California Riverside Center for Ideas and Society, and the Witter Bynner Fellowship from the Library of Congress. She has written eight books of poetry, one book of nonfiction, and a play. Her most recent book is *Look at This Blue*.

SEAN HILL is the author of two poetry collections, *Dangerous Goods* (Milkweed Editions, 2014), which was awarded the Minnesota Book Award in Poetry, and *Blood Ties & Brown Liquor* (UGA Press, 2008). Hill has received numerous awards, including a fellowship from the Cave Canem Foundation, a Stegner Fellowship from Stanford University, and a creative writing fellowship in poetry from the National Endowment for the Arts. Hill's poems and essays have appeared in *Callaloo*, *Harvard Review*, *New England Review*, *Orion*, *Oxford American*, *Poetry*, *Tin House*, and numerous other journals, as well as in over two dozen anthologies including *Black Nature* and *Villanelles*. Director of the Minnesota Northwoods Writers Conference at Bemidji State University since 2012, Hill lives in southwestern Montana with his family and is an associate professor in the creative writing program at the University of Montana.

BRENDA HILLMAN'S eleventh collection of poetry from Wesleyan University Press, *In a Few Minutes Before Later*, was published in 2023. Hillman has edited and cotranslated more than 20 books and has received many honors, including the Morton Dauwen Zabel Award for innovative writing. A former chancellor of the Academy of American Poets, Hillman lives in the San Francisco Bay Area, where she is a professor emerita at Saint Mary's College of California. Find her at blueflower-arts.com/artist/brenda-hillman.

EDWARD HIRSCH is a celebrated poet and a peerless advocate for poetry. He was born in Chicago in 1950—his accent makes it impossible for him to hide his origins—and educated at Grinnell College and the University of Pennsylvania, where he received a PhD in folklore. His books on behalf of the art of poetry include *How to Read a Poem* and *100 Poems to Break Your Heart*.

JANE HIRSHFIELD is the author of 10 much-honored collections of poetry, most recently *The Asking: New & Selected Poems*, published by Knopf in 2023. Her work appears in the *New Yorker*, *Atlantic*, *New York Times*, *Poetry*, *Orion*, and 10 editions of *Best American Poetry*. A former chancellor of the Academy of American Poets, she was elected in 2019 to the American Academy of Arts and Sciences.

GERARD MANLEY HOPKINS (1844–1889), a Jesuit priest and poet, was one of the Victorian era's greatest poets. He was an innovator in poetic form, experimenting with sprung rhythm and the curtal sonnet. Many of his poems celebrate the divine in nature.

MARK JARMAN is the author of 11 books of poetry and 5 books of essays and reviews. He is Centennial Professor of English, Emeritus, at Vanderbilt University in Nashville, Tennessee.

ROBINSON JEFFERS (1887–1962) was an important poet of the central California coast, with a keen interest in the environment, myth, and science. His poems, both lyric and narrative, juxtaposed his intense identification with the beauty of nature against a despair toward what he saw as the degraded condition of human culture.

WANG JIAXIN is one of the leading poets of China. As a poet, essayist, and translator, he has published more than 40 books, and he is the leading translator of Paul Celan into Chinese. His honors include the inaugural Ai Qing Poetry Award (2022). His book of poetry in English translation is *Darkening Mirror: New and Selected Poems*, translated by Diana Shi and George O'Connell, with a foreword by Robert Hass (Tebot Bach, 2016). Translator **ARTHUR SZE** is the author of *The Glass Constellation: New and Collected Poems* (Copper Canyon Press, paperback, 2024), selected for a 2024 National Book Foundation Science + Literature Award. A new book of poetry, *Into the Hush*, is forthcoming in April 2025. His expanded edition of translations of Chinese poetry, *The Silk Dragon II*, was released by Copper Canyon Press in the spring of 2024.

KHADJIAH JOHNSON is an Afro-Caribbean American comedian, food writer, and poet from Brooklyn, New York. Her work has appeared in *Vulture*, *The Best American Food Writing 2023*, *The Offing*, and more. She is a staff writer for the pop culture criticism website *Black Nerd Problems* and a contributing writer for Crunchyroll, and she hosts a restaurant and food column, *Scotch Bonnet*. Johnson has worked alongside numerous brands to help cultivate their voice for diverse audiences for worldwide distribution. From keynotes and culture critique to spoken word, her work has reached millions over the course of her 10-plus-year tenure in the creative industry. She has appeared on Epicurious and BET, and some of her pieces have been featured on the Emmy Award–winning show *Last Week Tonight with John Oliver* (HBO).

EVER JONES (they/them) is author of the essay collection *Transanything* (Curbstone, 2025). They are also the author of two poetry collections, *nightsong* and *Wilderness Lessons*. Ever is a professor of creative writing at the University of Washington Tacoma. Please visit everjones.com.

DONIKA KELLY is the author of *The Renunciations* and *Bestiary*. A recipient of a fellowship from the National Endowment for the Arts, she is a Cave Canem graduate fellow and founding member of the collective Poets at the End of the World. She currently lives in Iowa City, where she teaches creative writing at the University of Iowa.

YUSEF KOMUNYAKAA'S book *Neon Vernacular* won the 1994 Pulitzer Prize for poetry. His 1988 book *Dien Cai Dau* (meaning "crazy" in Vietnamese), based on his experiences in the Vietnam War, is widely recognized as one of the most important books to come out of that conflict.

STANLEY KUNITZ (1905–2006) was a beloved poet who served as US Poet Laureate in 1974 and again in 2000. In addition to writing poems and essays, he supported literary culture as a founder of both the Fine Arts Work Center in Provincetown and Poets House in New York City.

DENISE LEVERTOV (1923–1997) was a prolific poet and essayist, born and raised in England, who came to the United States and became an influential poet in the manner of Charles Olson's idea of "projective verse"—open-form poetry in which, as she wrote, "form is never more than an extension of content." Her poetry and political activism were prominent in movements against the Vietnam War and for nuclear disarmament.

ADA LIMÓN is the author of six books of poetry, including *The Carrying*, which won the National Book Critics Circle Award for Poetry in 2019. Limón is also host of the critically acclaimed poetry podcast *The Slowdown*. Her most recent book is *The Hurting Kind* (Milkweed Editions, 2022). She was appointed in that year to be the 24th US Poet Laureate.

DR. MANNY LOLEY is 'Áshįįhi born for Tó Baazhní'ázhí; his maternal grandparents are the Tódích'íi'nii, and his paternal grandparents are the Kinyaa'áanii. Loley holds a PhD in English and literary arts from the University of Denver and an MFA in fiction from the Institute of American Indian Arts. Loley is an inaugural In-Na-Po Fellow and a member of Saad Bee Hózhǫ: Diné Writers' Collective. Since 2018, he has served as director of the Emerging Diné Writers' Institute. His work has found homes with *Poetry, Pleaides, Massachusetts Review, Santa Fe Literary Review*, Broadsided Press, *Yellow Medicine*

Review, and *The Diné Reader: An Anthology of Navajo Literature*, among others. His writing has been thrice nominated for a Pushcart Prize. Loley is at work on a novel titled *They Collect Rain in Their Palms*. He is from Tsétah Tó Ák'olí in New Mexico.

OLEH LYSHEHA (1949–2014) was a Ukrainian Poet. Expelled from Lviv University in 1972 for his interest in contemporary American poetry, he was drafted and sent for military duty in Siberia. His first poetry book, *The Great Bridge*, came out in 1989. He was a Fulbright Scholar and was awarded a 1999 PEN Translation Prize for his *Selected Poems of Oleh Lysheha*, published in English by the Ukrainian Institute at Harvard University. His poems have been incorporated in theater pieces by the Yara Arts Group, headed by **VIRLANA TKACZ**. Tkacz received a National Endowment for the Arts Translation Fellowship for her translations of Lysheha's work with poet **WANDA PHIPPS**. In 2022 Lost Horse Press published *Dream Bridge: Selected Poems* by Oleh Lysheha in their translation.

ANNE HAVEN McDONNELL lives in Santa Fe, New Mexico, and teaches creative writing at the Institute of American Indian Arts. A recipient of a 2023 National Endowment of the Arts fellowship in poetry, she is the author of *Breath on a Coal* from Middle Creek Press (runner-up for the ASLE Book Award and longlisted for the Laurel Prize) and the chapbook *Living with Wolves* from Split Rock Press. Her poetry has been published in *Orion*, Academy of American Poets Poem-a-Day, *Georgia Review*, and elsewhere.

W. S. MERWIN (1927–2019) was the author of more than 50 books of poetry and prose, as well as many works of translation. From 1976 he lived in Hawai'i, where he restored a forest on land that had been a depleted pineapple plantation. A man of both pragmatism and spirit, he felt deeply about and wrote eloquently of the fate of nature. His many awards include the Pulitzer Prize in 1971 and 2009, and a National Book Award in 2005.

AIMEE NEZHUKUMATATHIL is the author of the essay collections *Bite by Bite* and *World of Wonders*, as well as four poetry collections. With Ross Gay, she coauthored the epistolary chapbook *Lace & Pyrite* (Get Fresh Publishing). She is professor of English in the MFA program at the University of Mississippi.

ALDEN NOWLAN (1933–1983) was an influential and prolific Canadian poet, novelist, and playwright. He was born into poverty in rural Nova Scotia, on a stretch of dirt road he later called Desolation Creek. He is the author of more than 20 poetry collections, as well as numerous plays and nonfiction works. His book *Bread, Wine, and Salt* (1967) won the Governor's General Award for Poetry. He also received a Guggenheim Fellowship and served as writer in residence at the University of New Brunswick.

Palestinian American writer, editor, and educator **NAOMI SHIHAB NYE** grew up in St. Louis, Jerusalem, and San Antonio, Texas. She has been the Poetry Foundation's Young People's Poet Laureate, poetry editor for *The New York Times Magazine* and *The Texas Observer*, and a visiting writer in hundreds of schools and communities all over the world. Her most recent book is called *Grace Notes: Poems About Families*.

LINDA PASTAN (1932–2023) is the author of *Almost an Elegy*, her fifteenth collection of poetry. She was poet laureate of Maryland from 1991 to 1995 and the recipient of honors, including the Ruth Lilly Prize and the Radcliffe Distinguished Alumnae Award.

CRAIG SANTOS PEREZ is an Indigenous Chamoru from the Pacific Island of Guam. He is the coeditor of eight anthologies and the author of six books of poetry. His book *From Unincorporated Territory [åmot]* won the 2023 National Book Award in poetry.

HAI-DANG PHAN was born in Vietnam and raised in Wisconsin. He is the author of the poetry collection *Reenactments* (2019). He currently teaches at Grinnell College and lives in Iowa City, Iowa.

FRANCIS PONGE (1899–1988) was a French poet whose intention was to write a new *De rerum natura*. He is regarded as a modern French master for his prose poems celebrating the language of things. Translator **C. K. WILLIAMS** (1936–2015), one of America's most respected poets, lived in Paris. His book *Repair* won the Pulitzer Prize in poetry.

IAN RAMSEY is a writer, teacher, and outdoor athlete based in Maine, where he directs the Kauffmann Program for Environmental Writing. His book *Hackable Animal* was a finalist for the 2023 Prism Prize for Climate Literature, and his book *Falling in Love with Mountains* is forthcoming in 2025. His writing has appeared in Terrain.org, *Orion*, *High Desert Journal*, and other publications. For more information, go to ianramsey.net.

PAISLEY REKDAL is the author of four books of nonfiction and seven books of poetry, including *Nightingale*, *Appropriate: A Provocation*, and, most recently, *West: A Translation*. She is the editor and creator of the digital archive projects West, Mapping Literary Utah, and Mapping Salt Lake City. Her work has received the Amy Lowell Poetry Traveling Scholarship, a Guggenheim Fellowship, a National Endowment for the Arts Fellowship, Pushcart Prizes, the Academy of American Poets' Laureate Fellowship, a Fulbright Fellowship, and various state arts council awards. The former Utah poet laureate, she teaches at the University of Utah, where she directs the American West Center.

ALBERTO RÍOS'S most recent work is a book of poems, *Not Go Away Is My Name*, and *A Good Map of All Things*, a novel. The recipient of the PEN/Beyond Margins Award, the Western Literature Association Distinguished Achievement Award, and a Rocky Mountain Emmy Award, and a finalist for the National Book Award, Ríos teaches at Arizona State University. He is Arizona's inaugural poet laureate, a recent chancellor of the Academy of American Poets, and director of the Virginia G. Piper Center for Creative Writing.

JEROME ROTHENBERG has authored or edited more than 70 books of poetry, including the influential anthologies *Technicians of the Sacred: A Range of Poetries from Africa, America, Asia, Europe, and Oceania* and *Shaking the Pumpkin: Traditional Poetry of the Indian North Americas*, books that established the field of ethnopoetics. His honors include Guggenheim and National Endowment for the Arts fellowships, two PEN Oakland-Josephine Miles Literary Awards, two PEN Center USA Translation Prizes, and the San Diego Public Library Local Author Lifetime Achievement Award.

MURIEL RUKEYSER (1913–1980) was an American poet, essayist, biographer, and political activist. She wrote poems about equality, feminism, social justice, and Judaism. The recipient of a Guggenheim Fellowship, she wrote a foundational work of documentary poetics, *The Book of the Dead*, a response to the Hawk's Nest Tunnel disaster in 1931 in West Virginia.

NATASHA SAJÉ is the author of five books of poems: *The Future Will Call You Something Else* (Tupelo Press, 2023); *Vivarium* (Tupelo, 2014); *Bend* (Tupelo, 2004); *Red Under the Skin* (University of Pittsburgh Press, 1994); and a chapbook, *Special Delivery* (Diode Editions, 2021). Her prose books are a postmodern poetry handbook, *Windows and Doors: A Poet Reads Literary Theory* (University of Michigan Press, 2014) and a memoir in essays, *Terroir: Love, Out of Place* (Trinity University Press, 2020).

sam sax is a queer, jewish writer and educator. They're the author of *Madness* (Penguin, 2017), winner of the National Poetry Series, and *Bury It* (Wesleyan University Press, 2018), winner of the James Laughlin Award from the Academy of American Poets. They're the two-time Bay Area Grand Slam Champion with poems published in the *New York Times*, *Atlantic*, *Poetry*, *Granta*, and elsewhere. sax has received fellowships from the National Endowment for the Arts, the Poetry Foundation, Yaddo, the Lambda Literary Foundation, and MacDowell, and currently serves as an ITALIC Lecturer at Stanford University.

DEREK SHEFFIELD'S books include *Cascadia Field Guide: Art, Ecology, Poetry*, winner of the Pacific Northwest Book Award, and *Not for Luck*, winner of the Wheelbarrow Books Poetry Prize. When he isn't teaching or editing poetry for *Terrain.org*, he can often be found in the presence of animals in the forests and rivers along the eastern slopes of the Cascade Range near Leavenworth, Washington.

CHRISTOPHER SMART (1722–1771), an English poet, was a major contributor to two popular magazines, *The Midwife* and *The Student*. *Jubilate Agno*, his best-known work, may have been written while he was confined in St. Luke's Asylum, allegedly for his religious mania. The poem was not published until 1939, when it was found in a library archive.

A. E. STALLINGS studied classics in Athens, Georgia, and lives in Athens, Greece. A poet and translator, her most recent collection is *This Afterlife: Selected Poems* (Farrar, Straus and Giroux), and an illustrated translation of the Pseudo-Homeric *The Battle between the Frogs and the Mice* with Paul Dry Books. She is currently serving a term as the Oxford Professor of Poetry.

GERALD STERN (1925–2022), poet, essayist, and educator, was the son of Eastern European immigrants. His poems are filled with outrage and tenderness, with links to his working-class roots and his cosmopolitan identity, to nature and to history. A recipient of many honors, his book *This Time: New and Selected Poems* won the 1998 National Book Award.

LINDSAY STEWART is from Glen Ellen, California. Her work has been featured most recently in *The Red Wheelbarrow*, *The Pinch*, and *Nashville Review*. Her debut chapbook *house(hold)* was published in 2022.

JONNY TEKLIT is an award-winning poet whose poems have appeared in *The Academy of American Poets*, *The Atlantic*, *The New Yorker*, *The Adroit Journal*, *Catapult*, and elsewhere. He earned his MFA in poetry from the University of Wisconsin-Madison.

KELLY GRACE THOMAS is a poet, writer, educator, and ocean-obsessed Aries from Jersey. She is the author of *Future Tense* (forthcoming from Alice James Books, 2026) and *Boat Burned* (YesYes Books, 2020). She is the winner of the Jane Underwood Poetry Prize and the Neil Postman Award for Metaphor. Thomas has received fellowships from the Martha's Vineyard Institute of Creative Writing and Kenyon Review Young Writers' Workshop. She is also the coauthor of poetry curriculums *Voices in Verse: Poetry, Identity, and Ethnic Studies*; *Stanzas of America: Celebrating BIPOC Poetry*; and *Words Ignite: Explore, Write, and Perform Classic and Spoken Word Poetry* (Get Lit), which are currently taught in the Los Angeles Unified School District. She is a Blackburn Fellow in the Randolph College MFA program. She lives in Benicia, California, where she teaches poetry workshops online. She is currently working on her first novel and memoir. Find her at kellygracethomas.com.

CRYSTAL WILKINSON, a recent recipient of a Writing Freedom fellowship, is the award-winning author of *Praisesong for the Kitchen Ghosts*, a culinary memoir; *Perfect Black*, a collection of poems; and three works of fiction—*The Birds of Opulence*, *Water Street*, and *Blackberries, Blackberries*. She is the recipient of an NAACP Image Award for

Outstanding Literary Work in poetry, an O. Henry Prize, an Academy of American Poets fellowship, a United States Artists Fellowship, and an Ernest J. Gaines Award for Literary Excellence. She has received recognition from Yaddo, Hedgebrook, the Vermont Studio Center, the Hermitage Foundation, and others. She was poet laureate of Kentucky from 2021 to 2023. She currently teaches creative writing at the University of Kentucky, where she is Bush-Holbrook Endowed Professor and director of creative writing. Her memoir, *Heartsick*, is forthcoming from Crown.

ROBERT WRIGLEY has published 12 books of poetry, most recently *The True Account of Myself as a Bird*. He is also the author of a collection of essays, *Nemerov's Door*. He lives in Idaho with his wife, the writer Kim Barnes.

ACKNOWLEDGMENTS

I am grateful to Hannah Fries at Storey Publishing for inviting me to edit this anthology. To work in service of the animal world is a pleasure and honor. I found surprise, delight, sorrow, and wonder in the works that came across my desk. The world feels richer in animal presence than it had without these works. I could not have curated this manuscript of poems without the marvel of the University of Arizona Poetry Center and its collection of more than fifty thousand volumes of contemporary poetry. My former colleague Steve Orlen called it "the best living room in America to read poetry." I could not agree more. Geramee Hensley offered invaluable editorial assistance, calling many new poets to my attention and attending with care to details of assembling the manuscript. Many thanks.

And bountiful gratitude goes to the poets who found so many inspired ways to celebrate and mourn and imagine their way into animal lives. You have opened dimensions of attention and care that we need. Thank you for your brilliance in a dark time.

During the months when I was reading hundreds and hundreds of poems to shape this book, I had the companionship of a particularly perceptive canine named Coco. Living with a dog means continuing a 15,000-year-old interspecies friendship. I treasure these years she and I share. I encountered other critters when I'd break from my desk: javelinas and coyotes on my daily walks; quail and roadrunners and verduns in my backyard; cottontails scurrying to avoid me; curved bill thrashers and mourning doves with their incessant songs; mule deer, bobcat, cougar—neighbors more likely to see me than I am to see them. Each encounter, no matter how quick, made me give thanks that these creatures still move among us. With so many animals leaving the world, every encounter is a gift. This book is offered in the spirit of reciprocation for such gifts. May we find our gentleness in making room for the marvels of Earth invention that share our animality.

CREDITS

Amirthanayagam, Indran, "Elephants." Copyright © Indran Amirthanayagam.

Aridjis, Homero, "The Creation of the World" Copyright © Homero Aridjis.

Baker, David, "Whale Fall," from *Whale Fall* by David Baker. Copyright © 2022 by David Baker. Used by permission of W. W. Norton & Company, Inc.

Bartlett, Brian, "Every Lion Until Now" and "Sloth Surprises," from *The Afterlife of Trees* © McGill-Queen's University Press, 2002. Quotations in the text are from *Marvels and Mysteries of Our Animal World* by Lorus J. and Margery J. Milne (1964); *Jungle Days* by William Beebe (1923); and *Wanderings in South America* by Charles Waterton (1825).

Bass, Ellen, "Grizzly," from *Indigo*. Copyright © 2020 by Ellen Bass. Reprinted with the permission of The Permissions Company, LLC, on behalf of Copper Canyon Press, coppercanyonpress.org.

——, "Ode to the Fish" from *Like a Beggar*. Copyright © 2014 by Ellen Bass. Reprinted with the permission of The Permissions Company, LLC, on behalf of Copper Canyon Press, coppercanyonpress.org.

Bell, Francesca, "Scorpion" from *What Small Sound*. Copyright © 2023 by Francesca Bell. Reprinted with the permission of The Permissions Company, LLC, on behalf of Red Hen Press, redhen.org.

Berry, Wendell, "The Peace of Wild Things" from *New Collected Poems*. Copyright © 2012 by Wendell Berry. Reprinted with the permission of The Permissions Company, LLC, on behalf of Counterpoint Press, counterpointpress.com. Also from *The Peace of Wild Things* by Wendell Berry, published by Penguin. Copyright © Wendell Berry, 1964, 1968, 1970, 1973, 1977, 1980 ,1982, 1994, 1999, 2005, 2016. Reprinted by permission of Penguin Books Limited.

Blaeser, Kimberly, "Buffalo Hair Fedora," from *Copper Yearning* by Kimberly Blaeser (Holy Cow! Press, 2019). Reprinted with permission of the author.

Bradfield, Elizabeth, "The Voice of the Manatee." Previously published in *Interpretive Work* (Red Hen Press/Arktoi Books, 2008).

Braziel, Tina Mozelle, "Drawl and Hum," Copyright © 2021 Tina Mozelle Braziel. Originally published in *POETRY* (June 2021).

Brown, Nickole, "A Prayer to Talk to Animals." First published in *To Those Who Were Our First Gods* (Rattle, 2018).

Clifton, Lucille, "the earth is a living thing" from *The Book of Light*. Copyright © 1993 by Lucille Clifton. Reprinted with the permission of The Permissions Company, LLC, on behalf of Copper Canyon Press, coppercanyonpress.org.

Coles, Katharine, "If Past Becomes Future." Courtesy of Katharine Coles.

Collier, Michael, "Boars Gleaning Through Cities at Night." Copyright © Michael Collier.

Corrigan, Brittney, "Anthropocene Blessing: Nightjar," by Brittney Corrigan. Courtesy of Jackleg Press (2023).

Cruz, Kamella, "Turkeys, Bucks and Bulls" by Kamella Cruz (formerly Bird-Romero).

Davis, Todd, "Carnivore," from *Winterkill: Poems* by Todd Davis. Copyright © 2016 by Todd Davis (Michigan University Press, 2016).

Deming, Alison H., "Prayer to the Sockeye Salmon." Courtesy of Alison H. Deming.

Derricotte, Toi, "The Minks."

Diaz, Jose Hernandez, "Tecolote."

Doty, Mark, "Little Mammoth," *Deep Lane: Poems* by Mark Doty, published by Jonathan Cape. Copyright © Mark Doty, 2015. Reprinted by permission of The Random House Group Limited and W. W. Norton & Company, Inc.

Dove, Rita, "The Spring Cricket Considers the Question of Negritude." Copyright © Rita Dove. Reprinted with permission of Rita Dove from *The New Yorker*, February 27, 2012.

Dungy, Camille, "Characteristics of Life" from *Trophic Cascade* © 2017 by Camille Dungy. Published by Wesleyan University Press. Used by permission

Empedocles, ["I'll tell you another thing"], translated by Dan Beachy-Quick, from *The Thinking Root: The Poetry of Earliest Greek Philosophy*. Copyright © 2023 by Dan Beachy-Quick. Reprinted with the permission of The Permissions Company, LLC, on behalf of Milkweed Editions, milkweed.org.

Fauth, R. K., "Playing with Bees." Copyright © R. K. Fauth.

Ferlinghetti, Lawrence, "Dog," by Lawrence Ferlinghetti, from *A Coney Island of the Mind*, © 1958 by Lawrence Ferlinghetti. Reprinted by permission of New Directions Publishing Corp.

Field, Edward, trans., "Magic Words," translated by Edward Field, from *Songs & Stories of the Nesilik Eskimos*. Copyright © 1967 Education Development Center, Inc. Courtesy of Edward Field.

Flynn, Nick, "Worker," from *Blind Huber* (Graywolf, 2002). Copyright © Nick Flynn.

Frank, Rebecca Morgan, "Not Everybody's Bestiary (Yet)" from *Oh You Robot Saints!* Copyright © 2021